Books are to be returned on or before
the last date below.

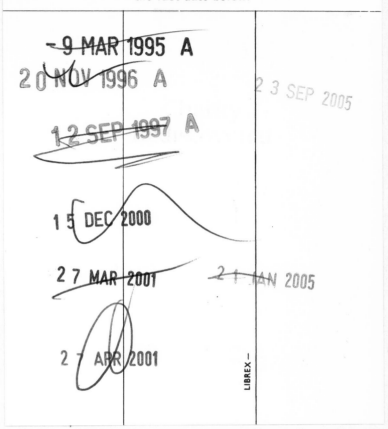

- 9 MAR 1995 A

20 NOV 1996 A

2 3 SEP 2005

1 2 SEP 1997 A

1 5 DEC 2000

2 7 MAR 2001

2 1 JAN 2005

2 7 APR 2001

LIBREX —

MARGARET SIMEY

Charity Rediscovered

A STUDY OF PHILANTHROPIC EFFORT
IN NINETEENTH-CENTURY LIVERPOOL

LIVERPOOL UNIVERSITY PRESS
1992

First published 1951 as
*Charitable Effort in Liverpool
in the Nineteenth Century*

Republished 1992,
with a new Preface by the Author, as
*Charity Rediscovered: A Study of
Philanthropic Effort in Nineteenth-Century Liverpool*
by LIVERPOOL UNIVERSITY PRESS
PO Box 147
Liverpool
L69 3BX

British Library Cataloguing-in-Publication Data
A British Library CIP Record is available
ISBN 0 85323 078 1

New matter set by
Wilmaset Ltd, Birkenhead, Wirral
Printed in the European Community by
Redwood Press Limited, Melksham, England

CONTENTS

PREFACE

This book was first published in 1951 under the title of *Charitable Effort in Liverpool in the Nineteenth Century* as part of the contribution of the University of Liverpool to the Festival of Britain. Apart from the fact that studies of this kind are rare and that it has long been out of print, there is an important additional reason why it should be re-issued, namely, that in the light of subsequent experience its relevance to our lives and times is even more evident now than it was over forty years ago. The book is not simply a period piece about the 'good works' of the 1800s. On the contrary, its concern is with the remarkable response of a developing urban society to the demands made upon it by rapid growth and change. The outcome was that the concept of the relief of poverty as a moral option for the individual changed to that of collective responsibility for the welfare of the community as a whole.

The contribution made to that progression by the men and women whose activities are described in this book was a vital one. Their numbers were relatively small, their power and prestige often negligible, yet their influence was such as to earn for Liverpool its considerable reputation for the practice of social reform. It is customary to attribute this to their commitment to the doing of good. However, though the charitable were certainly motivated by compassion (sometimes almost to the point of physical pain as in the case of Eleanor Rathbone), what eventually developed was something far and away beyond proposals for the relief of poverty.

Gradually, out of a patient process of trial and error, it became evident to them that what they were struggling with was not simply the problem of how to fulfil their heart-felt obligations to the poor, but the fundamental issue of the rights and responsibilities of the individual as a member of the community as a whole. What was required of them was no less than the exploration of the practical implications of mutual obligation as the basic principle of human society, given the vastly changed circumstances of life in an industrial city.

To the merchant community the presence of a great mass of poor people was an offence against God, but it also made a mockery of their proud ambition to win recognition for the city as the New Athens of the North. To the interlock of moral principle and sound commercial practice was added a unique awareness of the obligations of citizenship bred by the fact that Liverpool was undergoing unprecedented growth and development.

Seen in this light, poverty was as much a social and economic problem as a moral one and the charitable had to take cognisance of this fact, however reluctantly. Sheer force of circumstance drove home the further conclusion that in practice to 'love your neighbour' in an urban society must be so expanded as to comprise acceptance of responsibility for the well-being of the community in general. It was on this foundation that, by the end of the century, they arrived at the remarkable ambition to create a society in which it would be realistically possible for every individual without exception to claim the right to share in the common responsibility as an attribute of universal citizenship.

To this remarkable transformation women – and especially women of the rising middle-class – made a particular contribution. It is usual to speak rather patronisingly of their involvement in good works. In fact, it stood for a refusal to accept their exclusion from the responsibilities of full citizenship, a refusal which in the event proved to be a major factor in the drive for social reform. Out of their own need for self-justification, they stumbled on the fundamental principle that the individual can only survive through a relationship with others; the object of their charity was as much their own needs as those of the starving poor. The outcome was to infuse the drive for betterment with a passion for justice which, in Josephine Butler for example, reached such as intensity that she was forced to her knees to pray that she might be angry without sin.

Charity as the quality governing human relationships thus acquired a social dimension that was to inspire far-reaching political consequences. It was a concept that bore little resemblance to the one-to-one relationship of charitable tradition. Grounded in the sturdy assertion of individual conscience by the non-conformists, charity became a vigorous and vital agent for social change.

The relevance of this account of past experience to the situation in which we find ourselves today is clear. The setting-up of the Welfare State has removed from the backs of the charitable the heavy burden of under-pinning the survival of the individual. In the process the quality of love as a vital component in any human relationship has been strained to the point of near extinction. As a society we are deeply deprived of our right to give as well as to get. The vision of life in a caring community has eluded us. And without a vision, the people perish.

Never has there been a greater need for the voice of individual conscience to be heard than in these times of increasingly centralised government. The fight is on to win for us every last jot and tittle of our rights as citizens, but little is heard of the increased responsibilities that must necessarily accompany them. In the materialistic society of today there is a singular lack of the charity that translates moral outrage into the political will for change.

Where do we go from here? It is a truism to say that only by tracing the way we have come can we hope to discern the future. So to do must, however, be no mere act of piety. If we are to advance into the unknown world of the next century with courage and conviction, it is essential that we proceed on the basis of a thorough-going reappraisal of the past. It is abundantly clear that we have too readily accepted the denigration of the achievements of charitable tradition. Only by rediscovering the source of their inspiration will we be able to refresh our own flagging vision. Hence the choice of *Charity Rediscovered* as the new title for this book. It is the hope that this study of the motives and achievements of our forbears will contribute to that rediscovery and so enable us to set about the task of creating the Welfare Society of the future that surely justifies this reprint.

M. S.
March 1992

INTRODUCTION

SEEKING, for another purpose, information about the early days of
the Liverpool School of Social Science, I was startled to find that
the relevant records were hard to come by, and that this applied
equally to many of the associated organisations. The valuable
collection of annual reports and other material in the Picton Library
had been destroyed during air raids, and the chief source of information, at any rate as regards the end of the nineteenth century and
the beginning of the twentieth, seemed to be the memories of elderly
ladies who then were young. Starting thus with the modest aim of
recording information which was rapidly fading from recollection,
I found that I had lighted on an almost infallible form of escape
from the worries of housekeeping in the twentieth century, and one
in which, unlike the reading of detective stories, there has been
for at least three years, no turning of the last page. It is with a sigh
that I accept the inevitable ending of my task.

My own pleasure apart, I should have hesitated to embark on
a history of Liverpool's charitable effort, feeling that so high an
endeavour merited the services of a chronicler of far better qualifications. Miss Elizabeth Macadam, however, not content with herself
having contributed to the making of that history, was determined to
see to it that the story should be recorded, and it is entirely due to
the strength of her resolve that my recreation has been turned to
practical account. It was one of Miss Macadam's most endearing
qualities that her geese were always potential swans, and it was
her confidence which convinced me that my own efforts as a historian were at least better than the oblivion which would otherwise
be the fate of much of the material I had had the opportunity of
collecting.

The story is certainly worthy of preservation. Over and over
again, during the nineteenth century, the country looked to Liverpool for guidance and inspiration in the resolution of current social
problems. Nor were they disappointed. The situation in Liverpool
was exceptional: exceptional men and women were available to
tackle it, and the results were inevitably of profound interest and
importance. Indeed, so often was Liverpool's example a pioneer
effort that it becomes monotonous to mention the fact. The selfless
devotion of Victorian philanthropists to the forbidding task of
building a new society in the nineteenth century was nowhere more
notably demonstrated than in Liverpool, and it is as much to their
faith and determination as to the enterprise of the business man or
the toil of the labouring classes that the city of today owes its
existence.

I count myself fortunate that I was born in time to be a student

1

at the School of Social Science before this epoch finally drew to its close, for it is fast becoming past history. To the new generation of social workers, the daughter of the middle classes who had time to spare, the guilt of the prosperous in face of the condition of the poor, the self-sacrifice of the "typical social worker" and the leading part played by the voluntary associations, are old wives' tales, slightly comic as our mothers' fashions always appear to us to be, and nowhere made available for serious study. So fine a tradition deserves a better fate.

This is not a catalogue of philanthropic activity in Liverpool, for to have listed all, let alone give details of them, would have required a book in itself. Instead, I have tried to pick out those institutions and individuals who best illustrate the different stages in the progress of charitable practice and principle, so that the present can be seen as the outcome of the past, and contemporary difficulties are illuminated by the light their past throws upon them.

What then is the nature of this story, and what lessons are to be learned from it? Fundamentally the significance of charitable effort during the nineteenth century is that it provides a study of the early attempts to solve what is still the most difficult problem confronting modern society, the creation of satisfactory human relations within a community whose bounds are beyond compass by any single individual. The material problems of large scale societies have yielded to scientific treatment, and housing, sanitation, and other facilities for civilised living are largely reducible to terms of materials and money. That this should be so is due to the determination with which Victorian philanthropists sought to bring about improvements in the condition of the people. On the other hand, the technique of urban living, and the effective use of its amenities, which must be cultivated by the urban dweller if he is to be a happy townsman and not a miserably displaced countryman, have proved elusive in the extreme. Man has, indeed, been slow to adapt himself to the needs of industry, and unwilling to accept the way of life involved in urbanisation. During the nineteenth century, the organised attempts of the working classes to improve their condition tended to focus attention on their discontent, but evidence that the refusal to accept the prevailing conditions of life was common to all classes is provided by such movements as that for the emancipation of women, and by the consistent attack on the poverty of others which is one of the glories of the Victorian age. In so far as this dissatisfaction resulted in the improvement of material standards of living, the tale has often been told, but too little account has yet been taken of the experiences of the nineteenth century in regard to the problem of human relationships in an industrial society.

Perhaps most important are the lessons to be learned from the growing appreciation throughout the nineteenth century of the significance in urban life of the relationships between the community and the individual, as expressed in terms of social service. It has become an accepted convention to seek the origins of modern voluntary social service in the visits of the lady of the manor to the sick cottager, and the endowment of almshouses by the rich merchant. History does not support this facile conclusion. The "voluntary worker" is essentially a product of the industrial town of the nineteenth century, and "personal service" was a direct response to the special circumstances of life therein. The good works of tradition were based on the mutual and individual nature of the relations between giver and receiver, whereas the nineteenth century saw the development of a responsibility towards the poor as a class, which was neither mutual nor individual, but represented a dawning awareness of the need for a conscious relationship between the individual and the community. This resulted in the assumption by individuals of responsibility for the relief of the whole class of poor, a burden so staggering that only the intervention of the state could save the situation. Having begun with an inch, the state has now taken its ell. The voluntary society and the voluntary worker feel that they are being constantly forced to shift their ground, though often unable to decide where to shift to, or indeed, whether to give up altogether. Their present is precarious, their future obscure. One thing is obvious, that there can be no standing still, nor even any plodding on in the now familiar rut. It is the imminence of drastic change which justifies this record of what is rapidly becoming past history.

This approach to charitable effort as a study in human relations has, incidentally, simplified the task of selecting which material should be used and which rejected. Philanthropic work for the sick, for education, for the housing and care of orphans, for the redemption of the fallen, tended to concentrate on the provision of institutions and the necessary skilled staff, and though these objects inspired in many benevolent persons a spirit of generosity and public service which is beyond praise, it did not contribute materially to the problem of the relations of man to man. Moreover, it was in these forms of charitable work that the professional element and state intervention both made their earliest appearance, to the at least partial exclusion of the voluntary worker. The giving of alms on the other hand, remained determinedly individual, however much the principles of method and organisation might be applied to its administration, and the voluntary nature of the relationship between giver and receiver was always recognised to be of crucial importance. Thus though the activities of the philanthropic in support of institutions might, and often did, imply a genuine benevolence towards mankind, it is from the efforts of the charitable to establish relations of natural affection between themselves and others that we have most to learn. It is easy in modern society to find ways of being philanthropic but the practice of true charity has become a difficult and rare pursuit.

One or two points call for explanation. The title sounds strange to both the social worker and the social scientist of to-day, but it has been deliberately chosen because it typifies an attitude of mind which has passed away and which the young intellectual of modern times finds it hard to understand. An obvious difficulty has been the use of such generic terms as the rich and the poor, the middle classes, the churches, social work and personal service, which are handy labels, but liable to misinterpretation. I can only throw myself upon the mercy of the reader in this regard, hoping that my intentional meaning in each case is clear. In regard to the choice of dates: " One of the difficulties of an attempt to write the social as distinct from the political history of a nation is the absence of determining events and positive dates by which the course of things can be charted ".[1] The beginning was simpler to determine than the end. I have taken the beginning of the nineteenth century as my starting point because it was then that the revolutionary influences of the previous century really made themselves apparent, for example in the new forms of association such as the joint stock company and the philanthropic society, and in the new ways of living such as life in the suburbs and the slums. As for the end, my plan has been to take the story to the point where the first chapter of the next volume should begin, to make no attempt to tie the loose ends into a tidy knot but to lay them out in as orderly a fashion as may be, so that they can be picked up and pursued by the historian of the succeeding years. The turn of the century saw the tide set irrevocably in favour of acceptance by the community of responsibility for the material welfare of its members, and thus the inevitable end of the long struggle to express man's charitable affection for his fellow men in terms of material relief. A new interpretation of charity must now be sought: a new volume must contain its history.

I am deeply obliged to many people for their practical help, but even more for the implied belief that time so spent was not being wasted. Thanks to a particular few seem ungracious where the debt of gratitude is so widespread, but to some I am specially indebted, and I am glad to have this opportunity of thanking them: Mr. Priestley and the Liverpool Council of Social Service, Miss Saxton and the Picton Reference Library, Mr. F. G. Blair and the Committee of the Atheneum Club, Professor F. E. Hyde who read the book in manuscript, and successive years of students in the Department of Social Science who have materially assisted me by providing me with opportunities to think out loud.

Liverpool, 1951.

[1] G. M. Trevelyan, *English Social History* (Longmans, Green & Co., 1944), p. 551.

CHAPTER I

GENERAL BACKGROUND

THOUGH the individual histories of the towns of the North of England reflect the marked independence and force of character of their inhabitants, the process of industrialisation which they experienced in the nineteenth century was accompanied by social consequences common to all. In each, sheer weight of sudden numbers rendered totally inadequate every existing facility for urban living. The machinery of public health, from water supply to drainage and the disposal of refuse, in fact, the whole social structure including the care of the afflicted, and facilities for education and recreation, was called upon to bear a load far beyond its capacity. The final bottleneck, as always in similar circumstances, was created by housing. Their inability to pay for even the most modest of cottages forced upon the poorer classes those devices for increasing the rent-roll of each piece of property which led to the letting and sub-letting of every part of each separate house, and the building of houses on all available ground regardless of social decency or sanitary provision. Behind this bottleneck ponded up a flood of human misery, the stagnation of which created social problems so innumerable as to threaten the existence of the entire community. To absorb such a motley as was bred in the resulting slums, and educate it in the decencies of urban life, would have tried the resources of the most stable community, and this the newly industrialised towns certainly were not ". . . most of the big towns had the administrative equipment of villages ".[1]

Nevertheless it was less the slums than the life they lived in them which changed the normal mood of the poor from content to discontent. Bad housing, poor food and the physical discomforts of poverty were no novelty to them, but they bitterly resented the indignity of the new way of life in the industrial town. They resented the insignificance of their place in industry, their status as something less than full citizens. They envied the rich those opportunities for leisure and recreation from which they were themselves excluded by their condemnation to a life of all work and no play, an exclusion made all the more effective by the spread of the towns over what had been open spaces. Justice, religion, beauty, leisure, these were perquisites of wealth, and it was exclusion from a share in their enjoyment which constituted the real hardship of the poor, and provided

[1] J. L. Hammond and Barbara Hammond, *The Town Labourer*, 1760-1832 (Longmans, Green & Co., 1917), p. 81.

5

the ultimate clue to their attitude towards the wealthy. They became sullen under the pressure of the discipline to which they were subjected as mere muscles of industry, and their relations with their social superiors became correspondingly hostile.

Meanwhile, the middle classes were increasing rapidly in numbers and importance, and the atmosphere of promise and prosperity which surrounded them was in sharp contrast to the sullen discontent of the labouring classes, a contrast which was literally demonstrated by their withdrawal to the new suburbs. Yet desirable though the suburbs no doubt at first appeared, the rapid growth of the city drained them of individuality, while the increasing competition for employment turned the pleasure of keeping up appearances into a corroding anxiety. Loneliness and mutual exclusion set in, bringing with it a poverty of social life which, unlike material poverty, refused to respect the distinctions of social class, and indeed, became more marked amongst rich than poor. It is a measure of the failure of the new suburbs to satisfy the social needs of their inhabitants that at a time when the value of church-going was becoming increasingly open to question, life in the suburbs should yet centre upon the individual church or chapel. Almost the only means of satisfying the human need to belong to a comprehensible community, to feel respected and wanted by a group of people, was by membership of a religious body. This applied in special measure to middle class women whose lives were restricted to their homes.

This poverty of social life which applied equally to rich and poor was fed by the current emphasis on individualism. A man's first duty was to himself; the extent to which he should assume civic and social obligations was a matter he alone could decide. This view of man as an individual rather than a social being was supported by the current trend of religious teaching. Riches were the reward of virtue and their enjoyment was therefore the right of the individual concerned: poverty and hardship were equally personal, to be remedied by individual effort, or if beyond remedy, then nobly borne. Thus material circumstance, economic theory, and moral principle alike conspired to prevent the growth of new social relationships in the new towns, and it is only remarkable that in spite of it all, any civic pride, or corporate feeling, or even neighbourliness actually developed.

This general description was as true of Liverpool as of any other town in the industrial north, but with the important qualification that the town seemed to suffer all the common social ills in excess. It is remarkable to note how often, and under what varying heads, Liverpool could claim that while the facts held good of towns in general, they reached their maximum intensity in regard to Liverpool.[2] Poverty was more desperate, housing more squalid, social distinctions more cruel, the state of public health more shocking in Liverpool than elsewhere: these were claims which few other towns could dispute. Why should this have been so? Why should the normal pains of the Industrial Revolution have been intensified almost beyond endurance in Liverpool? The answer would seem to lie in the peculiar economic circumstances upon which the life of the town was based. All the usual associations of a small town with the economy of the country surrounding it were in Liverpool's case almost entirely absent. Its existence depended on the discovery and development of the facilities it offered as a port, and on this one means of livelihood hinged its whole fortune. It was to this fact that Liverpool owed its individual character and the peculiar difficulty of its social problems. What was elsewhere a process of the more or less gradual industrialisation of an established community was thus reversed in Liverpool, so that the industry preceded the town, and the town was only called into being by the demands of industry.

Hidden in dismal seclusion behind its marshes, Liverpool was hardly even heard of till advances in engineering made it possible to build there in 1709 the first artificial wet dock in the country to cater for the growing Atlantic trade. Until then there had not even been the tradition of administration associated with a parish church, for it was so paltry a place that its affairs had centred on the neighbouring township of Walton. The rate of its subsequent increase, however, far outstripped that of most other towns in the country. From the insignificance of 1700 with a population of 4,240 and a mere dozen or so of ships, it had by 1841 increased to 222,954 with a shipping list of about 4,000,[3] a truly staggering growth, which was thought worthy of remark even in those days of quick change. Lord Erskine described it possibly not ineptly in 1791:

" . . . I own I was astonished and astounded when, after passing a distant ferry and ascending a hill which overlooks the city, I was told by my guide, ' All that you see spread out beneath you, that immense city which stands like another Venice upon the waters; which is intersected by those numerous docks, which glitters with those cheerful habitations of well-protected men, which is the busy seat of trade, and the gay scene of elegant amusements growing

[2] For example, Dr. Duncan is quoted as saying " that the causes of the high mortality in Liverpool, both absolutely and relatively, will be found to be the same as those of towns generally, but reach their maximum degree of density in Liverpool." W. M. Frazer. *Duncan of Liverpool* (Hamish Hamilton Medical Books. 1947), p. 25.

[3] James Newlands, Borough Engineer. *Liverpool, Past and Present, in Relation to Sanitary Operations.* Paper read before the Public Health Section of the National Association for the Promotion of Social Science. October, 1858.

out of its prosperity; . . . all this has been created by the industry
and well-disciplined management of a handful of men, in a corner
of this island, since you were a boy' . . . This quondam village,
which is now fit to be a proud capital for any empire in the world,
has started up like an enchanted palace, even in the memory of
living man."[4]

The rapid growth of the town was regarded as a matter for congratulation rather than alarm. "This noisy, gay town, so full of
money and extravagance" was the description given by a woman
visitor in 1803.[5] There seemed reason to believe that left to itself,
out of the early expansion might indeed develop a New Venice. To
the tradition of responsible government founded by the small group
of governing families during the previous century[6] was added the
integrity and energy of those nonconformist families such as the
Croppers and the Rathbones, who found in its expanding commercial life that scope which was denied them in public life. Foreigners
were also attracted to Liverpool where representatives of foreign
business families were offered opportunities which would have been
denied them in the older trading centres. Such families frequently
brought with them a tradition of sturdy common sense and good
citizenship which was of the greatest value to the new community.
These various groups together formed a merchant aristocracy which,
in its appreciation of education and culture, its enthusiasm for
foreign travel (in the case of the nonconformists as a substitute for
university education), its handsome domestic architecture, and its
philosophical and humanitarian interests, gave some justification for
the comparing of Liverpool with Venice. The memorials of the
leading local families make pleasant reading, and the self-styled
merchant prince emerges as an attractive reality.

"It is difficult . . . to realise what a small place comparatively
was Liverpool of eighty years ago. It was the custom then for prosperous men of business to live as William Rathbone's father and
grandfather did, opposite to or above their own offices and ware-
houses, and on fine evenings they took the air sitting by the dock
side, while their children played at a safe distance from the deep
water. St. Anne's Street was then the fashionable abode of the great
West Indian merchants of the day, while Rodney Street was the new
quarter to which some of them, including Mr. Gladstone's father,

---

[4] Henry Smithers. *Liverpool its Commerce, Statistics and Institutions*
(Thos. Kaye, 1825), p. 17.

[5] Harriet Anne Whiting. *Alfred Booth* (Henry Young & Sons, Ltd., 1917),
p. 49.

[6] To which the Webbs pay tribute in their account of the work of
Liverpool's Municipal Corporation.   See Sidney and Beatrice Webb,
English Local Government: The Manor and The Borough. (Longmans,
Green & Co., 1908), pp. 481-91.

had migrated. Hope Street and Abercromby Square . . . now seem almost in the centre of the town, but they were then on its very border, and all beyond were fields and lanes. One of William Rathbone's earliest recollections was of flushing a snipe while gathering water-cresses in a brook running where Falkner Street (then Crabtree Lane) now stands ".[7]

But enchanting though such rapid growth may have appeared to be, it produced a structure sadly inadequate for the stresses and strains to which it was to be subjected during the following years. Its only social traditions those of the handful of local families and of the exclusive group of governing families who had secured control of local affairs during the eighteenth century, its administrative machinery and its material resources alike the product of hasty expansion, the new town of Liverpool was quite unprepared to cope with the boom which set in with the end of the Napoleonic Wars in 1815. Up till then, the expansion of the docks had been accompanied by a reasonable development of industries such pottery and watch-making, together with those based on the small whaling fleet, and on the curing of herrings for the home and West Indian markets. However, after peace had been declared, the unsuspected benefits of the Atlantic trade, especially in cotton, together with the rapidly increasing output from the hinterland of industrial Lancashire, so revived local confidence that the previous rate of expansion was not only restored but vastly accelerated. Eight new docks were built between 1815 and 1835. The demand for canals, roads, railways, offices and all the other necessary adjuncts for distributing the raw materials and finished products of industry was such that development and expansion took place on a truly astonishing scale, whilst the few alternatve industries suffered an equally drastic decline.

Liverpool became the Boom City of its period, the great emporium for surplus hands, greedy for men as labourers, indifferent to their needs as human beings. Here, if anywhere, the displaced persons of the times could find work, and to it they flocked throughout the century, impelled less by ambition than by their desperate need for subsistence itself, which their native place too often denied them. Some intended it to be only a step in the direction of the New World: to others it offered an opportunity for elbowing their way up out of the ruck of humanity: but in fact, comparatively few ever extricated themselves from the casual employment which was all the town had to offer. Countrymen from Wales and the North of England, peasants from Ireland, refugees from Europe, poured into Liverpool, forming each their own community, many bringing with them little beyond the habits of extreme poverty and an antagonism to the propertied classes. Poor, ignorant, often in a low state of health, the majority were totally unfit for the difficult task of adapt-

[7] Eleanor F. Rathbone, *William Rathbone* (Macmillan & Co., 1905), p. 56.

ing themselves even to the miserable standards of living already obtaining in the town. ". . . there are many, especially among the lower classes of Irish who seem to have no idea of a dwelling, except as a place of shelter from the weather. If it does this, they ask no more of it, and take little or no care to keep it in cleanliness or order."[8] Such codes of social or moral decency as they might previously have known hardly survived transplanting, and the restraints normally exercised by regard for public opinion did not exist in that polyglot community. The lack of employment for the young or for women, especially in view of the numbers of grass widows inevitable in a sea port, resulted in idleness which poverty and ignorance directed into habits of delinquency and brawling. The tradition of casual labour and the lack of alternative employment combined with the low standards of many of the immigrants to produce that thriftlessness against which the responsible classes waged scandalised warfare. A striking lack of stability and of the ties of neighbourhood and family loyalty developed amongst the labouring classes: the Domestic Mission noted in 1859 that probably not more than a quarter of its neighbours stayed in the same house or even in the same street over two consecutive years.

Standards were further depressed because many of the newcomers, especially the Irish, were accustomed to extreme poverty and were consequently willing to accept very low wages. In addition, differences of speech and religion tended to perpetuate and inflame distinctions which would have been better forgotten. All of which was intensified by the debauchery of soldiers back from the long French wars, and of seamen celebrating their first freedom ashore after the restraints of life at sea.

The census of 1801 revealed that 2,306 of the population lived in cellars, a sight then rarely seen in England.[9] "The numerous cellar residences strike a stranger with surprise, and the disgusting appearance which some of them present would give a most unfavourable idea of the town . . . However, if we compare them with those of the inhabitants of the polar regions . . . they have much to rejoice at ".[10] Dr. Currie, himself a migrant from Glasgow, commented as early as 1804 on the new and pernicious practice of building " houses, to be let to labourers, in small confined courts, which have a communication with the street by a narrow aperture, but no passage through them."[11]

The " mode in which this pestilential work was performed " was described by James Newlands, Borough Engineer of Liverpool, and the first such official in the country.

[8] Domestic Mission. Annual Report 1844.
[9] Smithers, *op. cit.*, p. 201.
[10] *Ibid.*, p. 373.
[11] Quoted *Porcupine*, 1 August, 1868.

"An ordinary street house, with fair accommodation originally, has had its lobby converted into a common passage, leading to the backyard. This passage is of course roofed over, and is in fact a tunnel from which the back room of the original house, now converted into a separate dwelling, has its entrance. The back-yard has been filled with new houses in such a manner as to leave only a continuation of the narrow passage for access, and from this little area of three feet wide, these houses receive the whole of their light and air. The passage has sometimes right-angled branches of the same size and is generally terminated by the ashpit, common to all the miserable dwellings, with its liquid filth oozing through the walls, and its pestiferous gases flowing into the windows of the last two houses.

This system introduced in converting one house into numerous dwellings, was imitated in the erection of new buildings."[12]

Although the results were certainly pestilential, the beginnings must have seemed innocent enough; the original intention was merely to utilize the back gardens and court yards of what had been better class dwellings in an effort to house the enormous number of labourers required for dock and railway construction at rents which they could afford. The housing of the working classes had never previously been regarded as an economic proposition, to be divorced from conditions of employment. However, in the get-rich-quick towns, rents were forced into a totally new relationship with site values which were themselves inflated out of all economic proportion by the pressure of population. The results were deplorable, not least in the evidence they provided of the willingness of man to batten on the needs of man.

"It is not that there are more courts in Liverpool than in other towns . . . but so freely has human life been sacrificed here, rather than that land should be *sacrificed* . . . that the average size of a court in Birmingham is twelve times the average size of a court in Liverpool; whilst in Birmingham no such thing could be discovered as a human being living in a cellar ".[13]

It was to economise in the use of land that the practice of building the court houses back-to-back was evolved. Simultaneously, as more and more people crowded into the town, and rents increased under the pressure of demand, letting and sub-letting set in to a tortuous degree. The provision of houses at rentals which the humblest could afford was quickly realised to be a poor investment, and the supply steadily declined throughout the century.

No neighbours these for the Liverpool Gentleman! Little wonder that those who could afford to do so, moved from the neigh-

[12] Newlands, *op. cit.*
[13] John H. Thom. *Sermon preached on behalf of the Liverpool Dispensaries* (Chapman Bros. 1845).

B

bourhood of such squalor: the handsome houses in Rodney Street of which one of the earliest was that of the Gladstone family, were expressions of this desire to escape from dirt and disease. As fast as houses elsewhere could be built for them, the merchant aristocracy withdrew from the river side, along which spread both north and south the line of docks with their attendant supply of labour. And after them, as far as their means permitted, went the office workers, the shop-keepers, the professional men, and the rest of the new middle classes whose rise was nowhere more dramatically demonstrated than in Liverpool. The housing shortage being already acute, it was equally natural that the labouring classes should crowd into the houses vacated by the well-to-do, however unsuitable the accommodation offered.

This spontaneous sorting-out of the population on a basis of social status was typical of that process of social disintegration which had become apparent during the previous century, but it was emphasised in Liverpool by the demands of the particular industry on which the town's existence depended. The construction of railways, canals and docks, and the handling of goods in transit, required a labour force distinguished by brawn rather than brain, while the whole machinery of commercial administration, including banks, insurance and customs, resulted in a disproportionate demand for office workers.[14] The master craftsman characteristic of Birmingham, and the Manchester man of practical working experience, could find little scope in Liverpool, whilst there was small prospect that the skilled artizan, attracted away from his native heath by the high wages offered to manual labourers, would ever be able to set himself up again in his own trade.

The inevitable consequence of this division according to the two main types of occupation was that the gulf between the working class and the rest of the community, typical of Victorian society everywhere, became a dominating feature of Liverpool life. Between the two classes there was little contact. Its slums were one of the least known parts of all darkest England. Friendly and responsible relations between master and man disappeared from the Liverpool scene earlier than anywhere else:

" In Liverpool, almost alone amongst the provincial cities of the kingdom, the intercourse between masters and men, between employers and employed, ceases on the payment of wages. This is a desolate condition of honest, striving industry, and bodes no good to the social system ".[15]

On the one hand emerged a people " from which the heart turns

---

[14] See page 50.

[15] William S. Trench, M.O.H., and Charles Beard, B.A., Minister of Renshaw Street Chapel, *Workingmen's Dwellings in Liverpool.* (1871)

in disgust which almost overpowers the feeling of commiseration "[16]: on the other, a regiment of office-workers whose sense of social superiority, whatever their economic limitations, was intensified by the lack of intermedaries between themselves and the mass of manual labourers. Those who rose from the ranks, or who failed to maintain their position in the middle classes were quickly dropped by their previous associates.

With the insurge of competitors for success and position in the years after 1815 the opportunity for founding the New Venice, if indeed it had ever existed, was finally lost. No one came to Liverpool for any other purpose than to seek their fortune; few stayed on willingly after the achievement of that object. The up-and-coming regarded Liverpool only as a stepping stone in the stream of life and consequently took no more interest in her true welfare than such a temporary stay excited.[17] It was regarded as a matter for satisfaction that so many of the leading local families were absorbed into London and county society, but the cost to the town of this draining away of those who might have been expected to plough back some of their profits in experience and kind was severe.

The newcomers lacked experience of wealth, and of the rights and duties which traditionally accompanied its possession. They admired and envied the poise and security of the established merchant families, but their imitation of them was falsified by a complete failure to understand any other way of life than that of the materialist. They in their turn were imitated by the numerous office workers, who, never able to claim equality with the rich, yet strenuously refused to acknowledge any relationship with the labouring classes. Hence the jibe against the " Liverpool Gentleman ". Their anxiety to maintain this distinction stemmed from the ease with which their own position was threatened: the vagaries of wind, weather, or international politics could rack the whole town with anxiety, whilst the risks normally attendant on the business of stock exchanges added to the general insecurity. Fortunes were made and lost with an ease which makes contemporary sketches of the lives of Liverpool business men read like notes for a work of fiction: it was not unusual for a man to be declared bankrupt more than once and rise again and again into the higher ranks of local society. The social effects were such as might have been expected: " Liverpool is the frightful example, or the *reductio ad absurdum*, of all snobbery . . . our Liverpool shoddy aristocracy . . . have no stability even in their own eyes, and they live in a constant terror lest any act of theirs might perchance cause a forfeiture of their own pretensions ".[18]

[16] Dr. Duncan. Quoted in Frazer, *op. cit.* p. 16.

[17] T. W. M. Lund, *The Ideal Citizen. An Appreciation of Philip Rathbone.* (1896).

[18] *Porcupine,* 11 November, 1865.

Porcupine, the satirical weekly of the last half of the century, described the insecurity and struggle of life in Liverpool as eating the very heart out of society, and leading to a worship of appearances which ill become a community "where every man, a grandfather at the very farthest remove, scooped a dock, or hammered a ship, or carried a hod".[19] The local measure of success was strictly economic; the local aristocracy was based on bank balances rather than blood. The materialism common to society throughout the country reached in Liverpool its highest pitch:

"Is there any community of civilised men and women in the world where all that pertains to culture of the mind is so little honoured, nay, is so openly scorned, as Liverpool? The pride of ignorance is rampant here. We say in all sincerity, and without the slightest wish to exaggerate, that the general public feeling of Liverpool towards the thinker, the scholar, the man of letters, the poet, is one of genuine honest, hearty contempt".[20]

Before the jostling of such aliens, what became known as Our Old Families inevitably tended to withdraw into the exclusive circle of their own relatives and friends, centring on membership of a particular church or chapel of a particular denomination. Their family trees illustrate to how great an extent these became closed circles. They maintained their status as local aristocracy by virtue of ancestry and education in a community where so many could lay claim to neither; they increased it by their activity in civic and commercial life, though the Dissenters among them were long restricted by the disabilities attaching to their nonconformity. This was the period during which the tradition of the Liverpool merchant prince was founded. In its application to charitable effort, the combination of shrewd and successful commercial practice with exceptionally lively principles of moral and social obligation[21] was responsible for a contribution to philanthropy which was to become peculiar to Liverpool, and was to earn for the city its reputation for outstanding leadership in philanthropic and social reform.

The long continued existence side by side of these two groups, the merchants with their acceptance of responsible leadership and the new middle classes with their materialism and their ambitions, was responsible for the curiously dual character of local society. The "old" were new enough in all conscience, but they wholeheartedly adopted the tradition of spiritual noblesse of the governing classes of the previous century. The "new" were genuinely a new

[19] *Ibid.*, 6 July, 1861.
[20] *Ibid.*, 27 October, 1866.
[21] See, for example, Robert Smiles *Henry Booth* (Wyman & Sons; printed for private circulation, 1869), p. 45, where it is emphasized that Mr. Booth and his contemporaries fought for the Railway Act as much for its benefit to the Lancashire community as for their own private gain.

class: nothing like them had existed before, and they had to evolve a tradition and a morality to fit their new position in life. The consequent duality of outlook was nowhere more evident than in their relations with the working classes, where the responsible humanitarianism of the one contrasted sharply with the sense of guilt of the other, with important effects upon charitable effort.

Meanwhile, the whole burden of cementing into a social entity this medley of people fell upon the religious bodies, who were no more familiar than anyone else with the technique of building an urban industrial community. However, they started with the advantage that to people newly uprooted from rural life, the mere size of Liverpool must have been daunting, and identification with some familiar group such as that of church or chapel a matter of necessity. Often the only source of help for the newcomer in distress, who by virtue of his " foreignness " was not eligible for help from local sources, was the charity of his fellow nationals, organised through their various religious bodies. Social life centred on the church and chapel: they were for many years the only socialising influence at work on the population.

" It is impossible to view social life without reference to churches and chapels, especially those Nonconformist ones where there is a deliberate effort to occupy the attendants so as to make them acquainted. For a vast number of respectable, intelligent, fairly prosperous families the chapel is *the only* social centre; its meetings the only approach to amusement, its friendships the chief road to desirable marriage, and often the chief source of prosperity in business. A steady young man commencing life in Liverpool, without capital or good friends, cannot do better for his own business future than by joining and becoming active, useful and respected in a large dissenting congregation. Whoever knows intimately the ways by which such have again and again secured public positions, or obtained capital when a good opening presented itself, or found a generous supporter in a sudden emergency, whoever has enquired what brought excellent maidens and excellent youths into happy wedlock, while thousands of others loudly complain that no choice of acquaintance is open to them, will confirm this ".[22]

Not least important was the influence of the pulpit as a source of inspiration to public service, and a means of educating public opinion, and it was the personality and leadership of outstanding preachers which provided " the key to the noble civil virtues of a number of our most honoured citizens ".[23]

In these circumstances, much of the practical work of social amelioration and reform was naturally associated with membership

[22] B. Guiness Orchard, *Liverpool Legion of Honour* (Privately published, 1893), p. 42.
[23] *Liverpool Daily Post.* 7th January, 1920.

of a religious body. Many institutions in the field of social welfare, especially those concerned with education and reformation, and many schemes for the relief of distress, were the direct responsibility of specific congregations, whose members gave support in both time and money. Almost the only machinery by which an outsider might penetrate Darkest Liverpool, was that of the religious missions. To women in particular these organisations provided that moral and physical chaperonage without which they might never have effected their first steps into the world outside their own homes.

Unfortunately, the churches and chapels were not able to repeat outside their own four walls the success which marked their work amongst their immediate membership. The old parochial system centring on an established church was not applicable to the masses of a raw town, and each religious agency had therefore to work out its own relationship with the people. The lack of any religious affiliation on the part of many of the poorest immigrants, the antagonism of the slum-dweller to religion in general, the expense of building and maintaining churches and chapels in the poorest parts of the town, the shortage of suitable staff, all combined to force upon religion the gulf which separated the community socially. Only the Catholics were able to secure any real footing amongst the working classes by reason of the large proportion of Irish amongst them, and they in turn were hampered by a comparative lack of support in the better-off sections of the community.

For this unhappy situation, the religious had themselves partly to blame. Ignorance fostered petty dissension, which the extension of the franchise to nonconformists in 1828 did little to cure, and the earlier years of the century present an unrewarding story of the perpetual fragmentation on points of doctrine of congregations whose contribution might more fittingly have been a demonstration of unity based on their common humanity. Augustine Birrell[24] gives an unlovely picture of the situation. "The inhabitants of Liverpool appeared to me to be divided between Church and Dissent by a wall harder than the wall of Balbus to leap over": [25] even within their own ranks, the Liverpool nonconformists were neither homogeneous nor harmonious, so much so that he thought his father would rather have seen him a convert to Rome than listening to the Unitarian, James Martineau. This was particularly unfortunate in that it led to a failure to overcome, even within each sect, the physical divisions of the population.

[24] For whose father the Pembroke Street Chapel was specially built when, as a testimony against "close communion" he left a Baptist Chapel in the town.   J. Allanson Picton, M.P., *Sir James A. Picton* (Walmsley, 1891), p. 162.

[25] Augustine Birrell, *Some Early Recollections of Liverpool* (Henry Young and Sons, Ltd., 1924), p.7.

This situation was not allowed to pass without protest from at least some of the clergy. For example, the Rev. A. Hulme, a zealous reformer of the Church of England protested that:

"It is altogether an anomaly, and a crying evil in a Christian land, that two communities whose members dwell side by side, within sound of the same bells, and under the rule of the same chief magistrate, should in many respects be practically as wide apart as if they resided in two separate quarters of the globe."[26]

Nevertheless, as long as the town went on growing, and the distinction between the social classes remained, the process of separation was a difficult one to stop.

"What is the history of half the Protestant churches and chapels in Liverpool? The original position of the congregation has been rendered untenable by the surrounding poverty and wretchedness, the old building has been sold—perhaps converted into a brewery—and the good people have erected for themselves a pleasant suburban place of worship. So religion is constantly trailing like a skirt behind prosperity, following it step by step away from the region where its comforts, its enlightenments, and its humanising influences are most sorely needed."[27]

Within the limitations of this mutual exclusiveness, many of these groups played an important part in local affairs. One in particular extended its influence over such a length of years and such a variety of interests that it stands out far beyond all the rest, though it is significant that even they were not known as Unitarians but as the Unitarians of Renshaw Street. They were not, of course, the only group of their kind, but they were certainly the most outstanding.

"Looking to the past, we see no other congregation— not even that at the Parish Church, or that at Great George Street Independent Chapel, or that at Myrtle Street Baptist Chapel, nor now even that at the Sefton Park Presbyterian Church—whose members could, and usually did, exert equal influence in Liverpool. During three-quarters of a century they concentrated and used with united purpose, an extraordinary amount of business influence, education and refinement influence, and the influence of that peculiar kind of sagacity which belongs to statesmen . . . no group of men, of equal number, has held together so long, or so maintained its high qualifications, or so consistently manifested far-sighted appreciation of great questions affecting the social well-being of the town, or worked with more dogged ardour to promote national education, middle-class culture, public parks, free libraries and museums . . . Whether the rising generation of the Rathbones, Holts, Jevonses,

[26]Rev. A. Hulme, *Condition of Liverpool, Religious and Social,* 1858.
[27] *Squalid Liverpool,* by a Special Commissioner. (Reprinted from *Liverpool Daily Post,* November, 1883).

Boults, Genns, and Bowrings, etc., will remain Unitarian . . . the future must show. But at present Renshaw Street Chapel, with its offshoots, is probably the greatest political and social force in our midst, although its best members are not often found on Boards of Directors or seen in the Wellington Rooms."[28]

How far this group owed its inspiration to the civic pride of men long deprived of the privileges of citizenship is a matter for speculation, but without doubt, the determining factor at Renshaw Street was the lead given by the Rathbone family.

"The chapel records show that his (W. Rathbone's) sons at once made themselves active as school teachers, etc., and thenceforth the energy, business repute, public spirit, platform faculty and wide-spreading benevolence of all of them gave fresh and increased reputation to the entire congregation."[29]

Generation after generation, this family displayed such remarkable vigour and energy in the pursuit of the joint ideal of their own and the public welfare, which were to them inseparable goals, as to justify the claim that "the further one inquired respecting this family, the more it became clear that the whole of the town's life was in one or another direction influenced by them for good, and that it had been thus for generations".[30]

The example of the Rathbones was outstanding, but it was by no means isolated, and the tradition of public service upheld by successive generations of the leading families was to become an outstanding feature of local life, and to earn for the city a reputation for zeal in philanthropy and selfless public service unrivalled throughout the country.

This then was Liverpool in the nineteenth century. "New wealth was in the pockets of new men. A new poor lived in new hovels."[31] The essence of the problem which was thus presented lay in the baffling nature of the relationship between man and man, and class and class, under conditions such as none had ever experienced before. Charity, benevolence, philanthropy, social service, these were the labels attached to the efforts of the rich to bridge the gulf between themselves and their fellow citizens, efforts which were themselves only part of the much more difficult task of constructing a new society upon the basis of life in an industrial town.

[28] Orchard, *op. cit.,* p. 43.
[29] *Ibid.,* p. 48.
[30] B. G. Orchard, *The Second Series of the Liverpool Exchange Portrait Gallery, being Lively Biographical Sketches of some Gentlemen Known on the Flags.* (Privately printed. 1884) p. 62.
[31] Anne Holt, *A Ministry to the Poor* (Henry Young and Sons, Ltd., 1936), p. 2.

CHAPTER II

PRIOR to the nineteenth century, relations between rich and poor had been precisely dictated by custom and habit. The poor were divisible into two categories. It was the function of charity to care for the reasonably numerous class of persons suffering from such misfortunes as sickness, old age, or orphanhood. The vagrant, the unemployed, and the generally thriftless, whose miserable condition might be largely ascribed to their own moral deficiencies, were not worthy of sympathy, and were therefore handed over to the harsher ministration of the Poor Law. Viewed in this light, there was nothing incongruous in the inclusion in the list of charities given in Gore's celebrated Directory of associations for the care of the sick, the lunatic, and the blind, together with the Institution for Recovering Drowned Persons, which offered rewards of one guinea for recovery, and half a guinea for each unsuccessful case, " to those who assist in taking up the Body, bringing it to the next Public House to where the Accident happened."[1]

By reason of its recent development, Liverpool in the early nineteenth century was deficient in such resources. Charitable funds of a conventional character did exist, but though fairly numerous, they made up an insignificant total, and were in any case, mainly directed towards the welfare of seamen and their dependents.[2] Outstanding amongst these was the Blue Coat Hospital for the free education of poor and orphaned children, which was founded in 1709; the School for the Indigent Blind, founded nearly a century later, still followed the pattern set by tradition.[3]

The idea of a charity specifically for the blind is said to have originated with Edward Rushton, whose own story has all the charm of the period novel, including a first voyage to the West Indies at the age of eleven, difficulties with a step-mother, and a dramatic rescue from drowning by a negro slave at the cost of his own life.[4] During a voyage to Dominica, malignant ophthalmia

[1] *Gore's Directory,* 1802.

[2] *Liverpool Vestry Books,* 1681-1834. Edited Henry Peet. Vol. 2. (University Press of Liverpool, 1915). Introduction, p. lxxxiii.

[3] Its records, including even the preliminary appeal made on behalf of the intended institution, have fortunately been preserved, and it is from these that the above account has been prepared, by kind permission of the late Chairman.

[4] *Poems and other Writings by the late Edward Rushton to which is added a Sketch of the Life of the Author by the Rev. William Shepheard Wilson,* 1824. His claim to have originated the School for the Blind is open to dispute.

broke out amongst the slaves: " Rushton, ever alive to the call of humanity, exerted himself beyond the mere point of duty, to afford them relief, and became a victim of his philanthropy. He entirely lost the sight of his left eye, and the right was covered with an opacity of the cornea. Mysterious Providence!"[5] After a somewhat chequered career, due largely to this zeal in responding to the call of humanity, he finally established himself as a poet and book-seller in Paradise Street, and was able to support a wife and family. He brought his suggestion of a benefit club for the indigent blind before a meeting of a literary and philosophical society in 1790. " The hand of benevolence, guided by the suggestions of ingenuity "[6] from Christie, the blind musician, amongst others, and the activity of the Rev. Henry Dannett, curate of St. John's, led to the opening of the School the following year. Nothing like it had been attempted before in England, and very little elsewhere. It was designed from the start to be less an asylum than a training centre. Occupations which it was hoped would gently engage the minds of the blind without fatiguing them, and at the same time help them to earn a living, included the plaiting of sash line, the weaving of worsted rugs, and rope-making of various types. The list ends abruptly with the comprehensive word " music ". Pupils with suitable talent were primarily trained for the office of organist, but could also teach music, and string and tune instruments: one Report appeals for gifts of harpsichords and pianofortes. To the criticism that this would lead to the streets being filled with blind fiddlers, the original Appeal replied bluntly that " violins are excluded ". This musical interest, together with the strong religious flavour of the School (one of whose Objects was to supply such a portion of religious knowledge as might reconcile the blind to their situation),[7] led to the building of a Chapel to whose services the public were invited. When, in 1851, on the extension of the railway from Edge Hill into the city, the School moved from the vicinity of Lime Street to the residential neighbourhood of Hardman Street, these services gained such popularity that the collections taken at them became an important source of revenue.

The story is told in detail because of the contrast it provides with the efforts of succeeding years. Belonging to an age when the word charity had still its own particular beauty, it is an admirable example of the conception of benevolence as an individual obligation towards those suffering an apparently unmerited misfortune, a conception which was to be so violently challenged by the new poverty of the nineteenth century.

[5] Smithers, *op cit*, p. 398.
[6] *An Address in favour of the School for the Blind in Liverpool*, 1811.
[7] *A Plan for Affording Relief to the Indigent Blind*, 1790.

However, there were already signs of a realisation that the changing circumstances of life in a new industrial town called for an adaptation of at least the methods of charity. A Dispensary was opened in 1778 which was specifically designed as an alternative to hospital treatment for the increasing numbers of sick poor. Apparently the earliest attempt to organise what had previously been individual almsgiving, was the Strangers' Friend Society,[8] founded in 1789 on lines which were to become classic. The committee consisted of prominent citizens, but did not include any women. Emphasis was put on the need for investigation to ensure that only the deserving might receive help, and the pauperising effects of charity be minimised. An earnest and rather shocked band of voluntary visitors met weekly to discuss their cases and allot relief. And underlying all else was the clash of method and principle with the feelings of human sympathy.

This Society originated with the Methodists, but was not designed for the relief of their own poor brethren, for whom a specific fund existed. Their attention was turned instead upon those who, not having been born in the locality, were accepted neither legally nor morally as the obligation of the town. It was greatly to the credit of the Methodists that they were so quick to sense the breakdown of the old vestry system; many charities found themselves hampered in after years by the stipulation that funds were to be allocated only to cases of local origin.

Another attempt to adapt existing traditions to new needs was the founding of the Ladies Charity in 1796. This was of importance because it was an exceptionally early effort to organise the traditional function of women, of visiting the sick poor which, as an accepted social obligation, was in danger of lapsing through force of changing circumstances. However, though the idea of ladies organising themselves for charitable purposes might be a novelty, their approach was strictly conventional. Admittedly " the marriage union, maintained in purity, is surrounded with sanctions lovely and of good repute; but the hour of childbirth, which succeeds, is an hour of sorrow even in the lap of luxury. In poverty, it calls loudly for compassion."[9] But such compassion was only merited by married women of good moral character and possessing the required qualification of local residence over a certain period of time. The immigrant poor, and the camp-followers, stood outside the scope of what could be expected of the charitable, and must seek help of the Poor Law authority.

This then was the position at the opening of the nineteenth century, a position displaying only symptoms of the troubles to

[8] Smithers, *op. cit.*, p. 275.
[9] Smithers, *op. cit.*, p. 272.

come. Difficult years lay ahead. Such was the reputation of the
new town that despite the severe restrictions upon trade of the
unsettled international situation, people continued to regard it as
a city of promise.

"From the maritime situation of this parish, the influx of people
from Ireland, and from Wales also, is immense. Our porters and
common labourers are chiefly Irish, those labourers employed at
the new docks and other public buildings are mostly Welsh. They
arrive with or without families, and the increased population of
Liverpool, between 1801 and 1811 being 17,268, must be chiefly
ascribed to these colonists. Few of these people obtain legal settlements, yet when distressed, or out of work, or in sickness, they
apply and are relieved by the parish."[10]

Trade depression and distress during the Napoleonic Wars only
served to emphasise the true condition of the urban poor, and to
reveal unsuspected inadequacies in both the quantity and quality of
the existing provision for the care of the needy. There was some
dismay and even fear at the relations which developed between
the propertied and labouring classes, and were gravely acknowledged to menace the very fabric of society. This was accompanied
by a dawning awareness of the changing character of poverty, and
a growing confusion between the proper object of pity and that of
the Poor Law. The distress of the working classes in times of bad
trade was accepted as a necessary evil, but the obvious degeneration of the condition of the poor was nevertheless deplored, as for
instance, at the town's meeting called in 1809.[11] At this meeting, a
Society for Bettering the Condition of the Poor was formed which
aimed at relieving the distresses caused by the severe winter and
the scarcity of food, by supplying the poor man with means of
earning "that one shilling which does him more good than two
which are given him".[12] Similar meetings were called in 1811 and
1812, at which funds were raised to furnish employment for the
numbers of able-bodied and to provide for other relief measures.
Various other societies catering for the new poor also came into
existence, designed "to promote industry, frugality, and order in
society, and to engender a certain strength or manliness of mind
among the lower classes, teaching them to look forward, with tremb-
ling, to the necessity of applying for parish relief, and to resolve by
self-determined privations in the hour of health and youthfulness, to
make provision for sickness and old age." [13]

[10] *Remarks on Mr. Joseph Dutton's Address to the Parishioners of Liverpool on Parish Economy and the System of Maintaining and Relieving
the Poor.* By Mercator, 1816.
[11] Thomas Baines, *History of the Commerce and Town of Liverpool*
(Longman, Brown, Green and Longmans, 1852), p. 538.
[12] Smithers, *op. cit.,* p. 305.
[13] Ibid., p. 307.

The situation in regard to the new poor was thus acknowledged to be confused and baffling but not more until the resumption of relations with France in 1814, and the opening up of trade with India and the United States of America. Thereupon "the dismals"[14] which had hung over the town for so long, vanished almost overnight and in their place set in a period of rapid development which, whatever its economic consequences, proved disastrous so far as social conditions were concerned. A small town open to all the winds of Heaven could risk taking quite a few liberties in regard to public health and morals, but very different standards were required by that same town when, thanks to its glamour as a city of opportunity for all, it became "a pool, into which want and ignorance and the lowest forms of life are continually flowing".[15] In face of the tide of humanity which flooded in,[16] orderly development was out of the question: " . . . the town appears never to have had the advantage of being planned at all; and the thirst of gain, operating unchecked at a time when the philosophy of public health was so little understood, has crowded our river banks with those ill-sewered and ill-ventilated mazes of buildings, which occupy the greater part of the lower section of the town, and in the local spirit of which there is so much that is prolific of evil."[17]

Of all the social consequences, most damaging was that by which imperceptibly the poor and the working classes were merged into one, so that the misfortune which it was the burden of charity to ameliorate was extended from the specific misfortune of individuals to the chronic misery of a whole section of the labouring classes. The consequent blurring of the old distinction between suitable objects for charity and those deemed fit only for the attention of the Poor Law officer created a no-man's-land which was to prove a source of worry and warfare throughout the century. The benevolent could no longer easily decide which of many applicants were worthy of help and which were not, yet the inadequacy of both their own purses and the coffers of the Poor Law to cope with poverty on its new scale made this a matter of the greatest importance. To this were added the doubts arising from the conflict between compassion for the wretched and anxiety lest the exercise of compassion contribute to their further downfall by encouraging begging and thriftlessness.

The situation was without doubt bewildering. The system of local responsibility for local distress required as its foundation a

[14] Baines, *op. cit.*, p. 568.
[15] Speech by the Rev. J. H. Thom at the Jubilee Meeting of the Domestic Mission, April 1st, 1866.
[16] In Toxteth Park for instance, the population rose from 2,069 in 1801 to 24,067 in 1831, and in the following ten years achieved a total of 41,180. (Baines, *op. cit.*, pp. 506, 629, 665).
[17] Domestic Mission Annual Report, 1844.

stable society with a clear conception of the rights and duties of its various members. This no longer existed, in the new port of Liverpool least of all, so that responsibility for the poor posed a difficult question.

The new type of industrial employer did not automatically accept the welfare of his employees as a personal obligation, the benevolent related their charity to their personal capacity to supply rather than to the demand upon it, and no one was responsible for seeing that the resulting provision was adequate to the whole desperate situation. To some, their eyes on their own material prospects, the situation of the poor could be shrugged off as calling only for reform in the Poor Law. To others, conscious that in some inexplicable fashion the increase in their own prosperity was bound up with the increasing misery of the poor, it presented an obligation and a challenge. Thus Henry Booth, engaged upon pioneer schemes for railway promotion which promised prosperity for both his family and his fellow-citizens, asked despairingly, "What hope is there, that if Liverpool continue to flourish for another quarter of a century, there will not be an increase of extreme poverty and wretchedness *proportioned* to the increasing wealth and prosperity of the town?"[18]

That the answer to this challenge might lie in the provision and enforcement of a specifically urban standard of living was an idea yet to come, though its seeds can be seen in the interest already expressed in schemes for improving the amenities of the town.

The resulting mood of question and confusion coloured the whole relationship of rich to poor, the Poor Law being constantly subjected to criticism and private benevolence continually goaded on to new exertions. Both discriminate and indiscriminate charity increased, and there was from 1815 onwards, a new enthusiasm for the formation of benevolent societies, themselves a novelty. These efforts expressed rather a general dismay than a particular attack, and reflected the variety of public opinion as to the method and purpose of charity. Their aim was primarily that of encouraging the labouring classes to accept with fortitude the conditions of urban life, either by moral persuasion or material relief. A profusion of Bible and similar societies was sponsored by the various religious groups which, regarding poverty as a moral condition, offered alms of a spiritual character. Benevolent societies were also formed to administer relief, usually on rather a limited scale, some according to membership of a specific religious or national group, others more generously, but all, in their anxiety to help only the worthy and upright character, typical of the contem-

[18] Henry Booth, *Thoughts on the Condition of the Poor in Large Towns, especially with reference to Liverpool,* 1824.

porary attitude towards the poor. The Strangers' Friend Society, already mentioned, was probably the largest, and its methods of administration became a pattern for them all.

Every effort was made to enable the poor, and more especially the fallen or helpless, to become self-supporting and self-respecting. Thus the Female Penitentiary was intended to "afford an asylum to females, who, having deviated from the paths of virtue, are desirous of being restored, by religious instruction and the formation of moral and industrious habits, to a respectable station in society."[19] Similarly, under the inspiration of a visit from Mrs. Elizabeth Fry to relatives in Liverpool, a Female Refuge was opened on Mount Vernon Green in 1823 to assist women discharged from Court or prison.[20] The traditional apprentice system had by then been partially and inadequately replaced by an assortment of free schools, which sought to combine the education of the poor with their inculcation with contentment, usually on a denominational basis. All that can be said of the result was that the boys were better catered for than were the girls.[21] Offshoots of the interest in cultural affairs then characteristic of the merchant-classes were two library schemes, a lady of the Roscoe family being concerned with that for Female Apprentices, but these efforts were regarded with some apprehension lest they stimulate discontent. The Mechanics and Apprentices were not allowed to read either party politics or controversial theology, and it was hoped "that a vigilant watch will be kept that few, if any novels be admitted; like deadly opiates, they steal upon the sense, and produce a morbid state of feeling, destructive in all ranks; but in the class of mechanics and apprentices more fatal than the deadly nightshade.[22] A number of provident societies and a Society for the Encouragement of Servants complete the list, this last making despairing efforts to improve relations between mistresses and maids, and lamenting the decline in the standards of behaviour of both.

Typical of the new attitude to the working classes was the almost complete absence of provision for their leisure time through philanthropy or otherwise.[23] Leisure was the perquisite of success and the conception of the lower orders as a working class barred them from any recreation other than that of the concert saloon and

[19] Smithers, *op. cit.*, p. 277.
[20] *The Welldoer*, January-February, 1909.
[21] Smithers, *op. cit.*, p. 264.
[22] *Ibid.*, p. 309.
[23] It was to be a long time before the provision of even the simplest amenities of life for the poor came to be regarded as a suitable object of philanthropy, one of the earliest efforts being that of Mr. Melly to provide drinking fountains, on which subject he read a paper to the National Association for the Promotion of Social Science at the meeting in Liverpool in 1858.

beer shop, which accordingly enjoyed a monopoly profitable only to their proprietors. Drunkenness in Liverpool achieved a degree unsurpassed anywhere in the United Kingdom and was long awarded a high place amongst the causes of poverty. It was no co-incidence that Lancashire became at this time the nursery of the new doctrine of total abstinence.[24]

To talk of benevolence in terms of societies is, however, misleading, for charitable effort was still decidedly individual. Such societies as were formed owed their main inspiration to individuals from the small group who took their social responsibilities seriously, and raised from amongst themselves the active support both in money and service, which then accompanied membership of a philanthropic committee. Private ventures, unsupported by a committee, were common. James Cropper and his wife, for instance, ran a farm colony, providing food and employment for all who cared to apply.[25]

So far as women were concerned, it was taken for granted that wherever circumstances permitted, they should exercise the virtue of charity, although in practice, they found their scope limited to the traditional sick visiting, and the care and upbringing of children: Mrs. Andre Melly, herself a Greg by birth, opened a small school in Smithdown Lane in 1822, for example.[26] Such limitation became increasingly serious, and the story of Mrs. Rathbone's share in the work of Kitty Wilkinson shows how charitably minded women of the upper classes had to set about their charity. Of Irish extraction, Kitty was brought up in the apprentice house attached to a cotton mill belonging to the Greg family, of which, incidentally, she used to say that " if ever there existed a heaven on earth, it was that apprentice house ".[27] Married to a porter in the Rathbone warehouse, she adopted various orphan children, and acted as Mrs. Rathbone's right hand in her District Provident Society work. During the first outbreak of cholera in 1833 she thus provided a natural point of contact between the Rathbone family and the fever-stricken. Though credit is always given to her for originating the scheme of establishing in her own cellar a wash-house for the clothing and bed linen of cholera

---

[24] P. T. Winskill and Joseph Thomas, *History of the Temperance Movement in Liverpool and District* (Reprinted from the *Liverpool Weekly Mercury*, 1887).

[25] It was typical of their intensity and thoroughness that their son John, and his wife, ate from " crockery of Quaker drab ", reputed to have been specially manufactured for James Cropper. Each article showed a negro in chains holding up his hands as he exclaims, " Am I not a man, a brother?", or " Remember them that are in bonds ". Frances Anne Connybeare, *Dingle Bank* (W. Heffer and Sons, Ltd.. 1925), p. 57.

[26] *Liverpool Daily Post*, 7th August, 1836.

[27] *Memoir of Kitty Wilkinson*. Edited by Herbert Rathbone, 1927.

victims, [28] there is reason to suppose that Mrs. Rathbone played an equal, though less conspicuous part in originating the idea, which ultimately led to the opening in Liverpool of the first public baths and wash-houses in the country.[29]

Intermediaries of such calibre were, however, increasingly hard to find in the welter of newcomers, amongst whom degeneration of character was almost inescapable and there were, in addition, the barriers created by the distance between suburb and slum, and the fear of what might lie in squalid Liverpool. Charitable work by women consequently tended to lose its individual character. The Unitarians, for example, formed a Ladies' Committee in 1821 in connection with their charity schools, which only supervised the work: their minutes record that Ellen B. was brought before them for telling untruths, and that Betsy and Sarah F. had left school because the mistress had cut their hair short in front.[30] The Liverpool City Mission,[31] which originated in 1829 as the Liverpool Christian Instruction Society, early formed a Ladies' Association, but the only function specifically allotted to it was that of raising money.[32]

As to premises, it is interesting to discover that even at this early date, social work was conducted in an atmosphere of adapted gentility. In 1830, the Liverpool Night Asylum for the Houseless Poor was opened as a permanent shelter to replace that provided as an emergency measure in the vacant Guard House in Chapel Street.

" There is, in Freemason's-row, a large double house, with a spacious yard in front, formerly a garden; and as the premises were unsuitable for respectable tenants, on account of being in the immediate vicinity of the most indigent part of the Liverpool population, a very advantageous bargain was made with the proprietors; and, on consideration of thirty pounds, the tenant (who kept carts and cars) consented to quit possession on the 10th of August, 1830, and the premises, which were in the most dilapidated condition, were put into thorough repair, at a very considerable expense, as there was little or nothing left standing except the doors and windows ".[33]

[28] Kitty Wilkinson was presented in 1846 with a silver teapot inscribed as being from " The Queen, the Queen Dowager, and the Ladies of Liverpool ".
[29] Private Memoir of William Rathbone. Kindly lent by Mrs. Hugh Rathbone.
[30] Geo. Eyre Evans, *A History of Renshaw Street Chapel, Liverpool* (C. Green and Son, 1887), p. 85.
[31] See page 33.
[32] Alex Armstrong, F.R.G.S., *These Four Score Years* (Liverpool City Mission, MCMIX).
[33] *Description of the Liverpool Night Asylum for the Houseless Poor*, 1839.

Illustrations show a man in tails and breeches, apparently most comfortably installed on the sloping bunks with which the house and stables were fitted. This asylum was, incidentally, a pioneer effort, the first of its kind in the country.

The story was to be repeated over and over again; few Liverpool charities have been able to afford premises designed for their specific purposes and the process whereby charity thus filled the shoes of departing gentry may, perhaps, be taken as symbolic of the theme of this book.

From time to time attempts were made to co-ordinate this medley of effort and introduce something like order into charitable affairs. As early as 1810, Edgar Corrie, a retired merchant, had advocated action against the ill effects of indiscriminate charity, urging its organization on the division of the town into districts.[34]

A modest example of joint effort in 1822, was Lady Derby's Benevolent Society or Annual Sale of Ornamental and Fancy Works, prepared by ladies for the purpose. " On this occasion, her Ladyship, with many other ladies of respectability, become shopkeepers for the day, and sell articles to purchasers. The proceeds were divided amongst different charities, at the discretion of the committee of ladies ".[35] The Society unhappily got into difficulties with the professional sewing women, who resented the competition of ladies of leisure. Nor were her Ladyship's powers of co-ordination extended to include Dissenters, who appear to have organised their own Bazaar. A project of wider scope the early promise of which unfortunately did not mature was the Charitable Institution House built by John Gladstone, James Cropper, and Samuel Hope in 1820. Their intention was that rooms in the House should be available free of charge for the use of " all charitable institutions calculated to promote either the religious or moral improvement of their fellow creatures without regard to any distinction of sect or denomination ".[36] Offices were made available for the Ladies' Branch of the Bible Society, the Liverpool Marine Bible Society, and three other societies which were shortly to be formed " for the purpose of collecting reports and records of charitable institutions, and for the purpose of encouraging the reading of publications calculated to promote the moral and religious improvement of the lower classes of Society ". It was here, for instance, that the meeting was held in 1820 at which the Association for Superseding the use of Boys in Sweeping Chimneys was formed.

[34] Edgar Corrie, *Letters on the Subject of Bettering the Condition and Increasing the Comforts of the Poor in the Town and neighbourhood of Liverpool,* 1810.

[35] Smithers, *op. cit.,* p. 293.

[36] Copy of the Trust Deeds lent by the Y.W.C.A., the present tenants.

There was all the more need for some organisation of alms-giving because the removal of the prosperous to the outer fringes of the town caused the beggars to shift their attendance from the mistress at her back-door, where their claims were to a certain extent verifiable, to the master in his office to whom they were simply a mob. William Rathbone, always an earnest advocate of the application of business method to benevolence, described how, when he first entered his father's office in 1835 he found that the numbers of applicants for charity were a serious nuisance. His father, he says, "held very sound opinions on the subject of the evil done to character by relief given without sufficient knowledge, but being very tender-hearted, he could seldom resist sweetening his lectures on the duty of self-reliance by a shilling or half-a-crown. At his son's suggestion he consented to refer all applicants to the office of a local relief society, with instructions to make strict enquiries and to give substantial help when desirable. At the end of a month or two the office was almost cleared of appli-cants, and of those that persisted so few stood the test of investiga-tion that the amount disbursed on his behalf by the charitable society was under £5 a year ".[37]

Although local historians, anxious to create a favourable im-pression of the new town, pointed to all this activity as satisfactory proof of the town's philanthropic zeal, relations between the classes continued to deteriorate. The antagonism and resentment of the poor were rightly viewed with anxiety and fear, and the problems of charity in the literal sense of who should be given what and how much, became inextricably confused with the fundamental question of the human relationship involved between givers and receivers, no longer as individuals but as classes. "The rich . . . present themselves to the poor as a distinct and separate caste,— *as the rich*; while the poor are merely regarded—*as the poor*."[38] Such a marshalling of society into opposing forces was viewed with apprehension, the more so because the bridge across the gulf between rich and poor which charity had previously provided was now ceasing to function.

"Even those countless institutions which benevolence has everywhere set on foot for the relief of poverty and distress and disease, comparatively speaking, do but little towards awakening a brotherly feeling between the various ranks of society. The rich are givers under the impulse of abstract charity, without knowing the particular persons to whom their assistance will be extended.

---

[37] E. Rathbone, *op. cit.,* p. 128.

[38] Rev. James Aspinall, *A Sermon preached at St. Michael's Church, Liver-pool, on Sunday, April, 8th, 1830, upon the subject of the Provident District Society now forming in that town.*

On both sides the connecting links of love and interest, the sympathy, are wanting."[39]

The founders of the District Provident Society showed a surprising grasp of the situation when they declared boldly in 1829 that whilst the ultimate aim must be the elevation of the moral sense of the poor, " it is very difficult, *humanly speaking,* to preach Christianity with any effect, to men and women, who have no comforts, and seemingly no desire for any, who live with, and like pigs in miserable, wet, unwholesome cellars, hot beds of disease, without any provisions for the next meal or money to buy any. It seems an almost hopeless attempt to argue with people respecting the wants of a future life, when they never think of providing for those of the following day ".[40]

The practical implications of their statement eluded them however. The only hope of dealing with the threatening mass of poverty lay, the Society decided (and it was on this that their claim to superiority over existing agencies rested), in the development of regular communications of friendly intercourse between rich and poor. The Society's agent claimed that, " a word spoken in season every week by a rich person to a poor person, will do more to reclaim him from reckless improvidence and low debauchery than any other *human* expedient that I am acquainted with ".[41] Ingeniously combining all its objects in one scheme, the District Provident Society dispensed advice and Bibles, offered material encouragement in the shape of relief and a premium of sixpence on every ten shillings saved, and facilitated contacts between the classes by relying for the bulk of its workers on voluntary District Visitors. The Society began its work in 1829[42] and quickly secured over two hundred helpers, who were organised into twenty-one District Committees, working under a General Committee of great local prestige. Its efforts resulted in considerable annual savings, but so conscious were its sponsors of the mendicity and worthlessness of many of the poor, that the Society tended to become one for the suppression of vice rather than the promotion of virtue. Relations between agents and clients under such conditions could hardly be expected to prosper. Visitors were warned that they must expect to meet with, in the course of their visiting, " poverty and distress in their most fearful shapes. . . . You will have to contend with that fierce spirit of independence, which will brook nothing that it may regard as an influence with

---

[39] *Ibid.*

[40] *An account of the Liverpool District Provident Visiting Society* by James Shaw, Agent, Liverpool, 1834.

[41] *Ibid.*

[42] J. A. Picton, *Memorials of Liverpool,* Vol. I, p. 484 (Longmans, Green and Co., 1873).

its affairs, which will look upon a word of advice as a word unseasonably spoken, and will force you from its habitation in that decided manner which will plainly tell you never to enter there again. . . . But, mark me, if you encounter such things to discourage you, the pleasurable feelings in store for you in the exercise of your duty, which will more than counterbalance all the pain they will inflict, will cheer you in your path, and incite you to persevere ".[43] And the poor were exhorted to receive the visitors kindly, since their intention "flows from that pure feeling of benevolence, which has founded so many charities for your temporal wants."

In their anxiety to discountenance mendicity, careful instructions were issued to each volunteer, reminding them that it would be as much their province to detect imposition as to relieve distress and no less than five forms were provided on which to record the progress of each case from improvidence to thrift. Of the resulting "Charitable Police" the Society's agent remarked, in a brochure prepared for the guidance of many who sought to follow Liverpool's example, that it would be difficult to exaggerate the probable benefits. Amongst these, however, an increase of brotherly love was not necessarily to be found. Subsequent annual reports stress the importance of turning the "Society into a field where the rich and poor may meet together to do honour to 'the Lord who is Maker of them all';"[44] but the progress actually reported consists entirely of amounts saved, of relief given, of imposture exposed.

Meanwhile, the glut of labour had so inflated the ranks of the poor that the problem of reforming them by individual effort or even of effecting any sort of personal contact with them was one of the greatest practical difficulty, to meet which there had been no corresponding increase in the quality or numbers of those available to undertake such work.

"I am aware," said the Rev. John Thom, "how distrustful many have been made by the results of their own experience of the efficacy of visits to the poor . . . made languidly by people little fervid or earnest, who deem themselves very good and gracious for taking so much trouble, and the poor very ungrateful for not being overpowered by their kindness, whilst at the same time they are hardly more than present in body with their hearts and their chiefest interests elsewhere."[45]

Not only was doubt expressed as to the value of "visiting the poor", but the accepted idea that it was the proper function of

[43] Aspinall, *op. cit.*
[44] Annual Report, 1831.
[45] Rev. J. H. Thom, *Sermon on the Necessity for a Ministry in Special Adaptation to the Poor*, Christmas Day, 1835.

charity to meet their material needs was also subjected to increasing criticism.

"In the first place, I would briefly advert to the influence of over-numerous public charities upon the conduct and happiness of the lower working classes of this town. Having observed their general effects with as much attention as was in my power, I can rest upon no other conclusion than that, though at their first institution they may possibly do more good than evil, they usually issue, in proportion to the scale of their means and operations, in doing far more evil than good. I fear this is an hard saying, and that there are few who can hear it. I make the statement only from a strong sense of duty and responsibility. To the administration of more than one of the local charities, I am always ready to pay a tribute of merited praise; but nothing, I fear, can take from their natural tendency to propagate the very evils they were intended to counteract. While they exist, there will always, I think, be one great source of dependency and degradation among the lower classes of the poor."[46]

Such a statement reflects a hardening of public opinion in regard to the treatment of the poor. The situation was still extremely confused, but there was at least common agreement that poverty had somehow got out of hand, and called for emergency measures. On the one hand, there was increasing support for the conception of the Poor Law as a deterrent which, under the Act of 1834, made it a crime to be poor in England:[47] on the other, as an obvious corollary, was the growing conviction that the purpose of charity was to help the "deserving" to keep out of poverty. Poverty being regarded as essentially a moral condition, charity must therefore be directed to rousing in the individual a desire for a virtuous and upright life rather than to the relief of material want. Translated into practical terms, this meant devising some way of overcoming the indifference and even antagonism of the poor towards the means of their salvation as presented to them by existing forms of religious organisation. To this problem, the more thoughtful amongst the charitable therefore turned their attention.

[46] Domestic Mission Annual Report, 1838.

[47] Disraeli quoted in Frank J. Bruno, *Trends in Social Work* (Columbia University Press, 1948), p. 70.

CHAPTER III

THE CHALLENGE OF THE NEW POOR: (i) THE RESPONSE OF " PURE FAITH ", 1830-1850.

NUMEROUS small societies were already concerned with the supply of spiritual nourishment to the people, but the first evidence of any real sense of urgency in such work was the meeting of a group of leading citizens at the Charitable Institution House in 1829 to form a Society for the Promotion of the Religious Instruction of the Poor.[1] It is a tribute to the strength of the sense of social obligation of its founders, that the Society was organised on an inter-denominational basis, and that its seventeen missioners were able to secure wide acceptance as extra-mural servants of the churches as a whole. The object of the Society was strictly confined to the revival of religious vitality amongst the poor: its progress was measured in terms of holy living and "hopeful" dying. Of the trial of strength which must have occurred when faith encountered the obstacles to grace presented by extremes of material poverty, no record remains, beyond such occasional references as that to the Missioner who was disqualified from labour in the late 'forties by acute mental dejection.

Fortunately a detailed account of just such a trial of strength is available in the annual reports of the very similar Mission to the Poor set up by the Unitarians some years later. This provides an admirable illustration of the reaction to their times of a group of people distinguished for their social sensibility, and is all the more valuable in that it reflects the drastic change which pressure of circumstances forced upon charitable theory and practice.

The Unitarians in Liverpool were habitual philanthropists but their immediate inspiration they undoubtedly owed to the appointment of James Martineau to the Paradise Street Chapel in 1832 and more particularly, of John Hamilton Thom to the Renshaw Street Chapel in the previous year.[2]

"Mr. Thom was only twenty-three years old, and the congregation he had to face numbered among its members men and women who were in their several ways leaders in the political, civic and literary life of the town. Their own earnestness of conviction and of life made them perhaps the better able to appreciate unusual power in others, and Mr. Thom's influence among them

---

[1] Subsequently known as the Liverpool City Mission.

[2] Chapels which in due course followed the movement of population to Hope Street and Ullet Road respectively.

soon became unique and profound. His following was never a
large one, for although he had some of the best qualities of an
orator, his sermons made too great a demand upon the attention
and spiritual thoughtfulness of his hearers to suit the mass of
churchgoers."[3]

Thom became one of the chief influences on charitable affairs
in Liverpool, all the more so because in 1838 he married Hannah
Mary, daughter of William Rathbone. Their marraige was the
first celebrated in the Renshaw Street Chapel under the Dissenters
Marriage Act, and "the large family connexion of the bride, the
fact that her father was then Mayor of Liverpool, the public
eminence of the bridegroom, and the novelty of the scene in a
chapel, brought together a considerable congregation."[4]

Thom's conception of charity was essentially a concern for the
morally impoverished, and the stress he laid upon the necessity
of each individual amongst his congregation accepting an active
responsibility for the relief of such poverty led William Rathbone
to say of him that his particular contribution lay in the appeal he
made to the individual conscience, and the awareness he roused
in others of unsuspected obligations.[5]

Yet though Thom's preaching roused in his hearers this sense
of unsuspected obligations, what they ought to do about it presented a considerable practical problem. It is difficult now to
grasp how real the conception of Darkest England was for the
nineteenth century, even before the actual phrase had been coined.
Liverpool's slums were regarded as foreign territory into which
only doctors or ministers of religion might normally venture. The
reports from men who undertook to work amongst the poor read,
in fact, like those of veritable missionaries, men as conscious of
being pioneers and explorers as were their colleagues abroad.
Even the nature of the relationship to be established with the
new poor was unknown. The philanthropic patronage of the
eighteenth century was in process of being discarded, but what
human relationship, what technique of effecting contact between
man and man, was to replace it, was a matter awaiting the solution of experience. It had even been doubted whether the inhabitants of the slums were of the same stuff as the rest of humanity,
or whether being obviously bestial, they were beyond redemption.
That such ideas should have been entertained in regard, not to a
minority but to the great mass of the industrial classes is a forbidding thought which vastly increases one's respect for the courage

---

[3] E. Rathbone, *op. cit.*, p. 165.

[4] John Hamilton Thom, *A Spiritual Faith.* Memorial Preface by James
Martineau (Longmans, Green and Co., 1895), p. xviii.

[5] E. Rathbone, *op. cit.*, p. 65.

and moral stamina of those who, like Thom and his contemporaries, set out to prove the contrary.

To the Unitarians all this provided no excuse for inactivity. On the contrary it added the zest of opposition to the zeal with which they sought for suggestions as to how to put their ideas into operation. Despairing of inspiration at home, they looked abroad, as a merchant community such as theirs might be expected to do; and writing thirty years after the event, James Martineau was still moved by the memory of the quickened interest with which they heard of the work of the Rev. Joseph Tuckerman in Boston, U.S.A. When he came to England Dr. Tuckerman and his travelling companion were invited to visit the Rathbones at "Greenbank". "Their benevolent and devout enthusiasms came upon us like the angel descending to stir the sleeping waters, and their recital of what was being done to uplift and evangelise the neglected classes in Boston fell as a convicting and converting word, and yet a word of hope and zeal, upon our conscience, and not least on that of Mr. Thom."[6]

On Christmas Day, 1835, Thom preached twice at Renshaw Street on "The Necessity for a Ministry in Special Adaptation to the Poor", his sermons suggesting that considerable thought had been given to the practical implications of such a ministry.[7] But there was inspiration as well as careful preparation behind his words. His argument was based on the sound principle that it is the condition of their poor which determines the morality of a people, and that morality itself is not a human attribute but one which must be preached. The even sounder practice was enunciated that "before [the poor] will go in quest of [the gospel] they must feel a want of it—a desire of the spiritual affections for spiritual nourishment. . . . The most degraded are always the most contented with their lot, for to know little is to have few desires."[8] Such rousing of the need for spiritual nourishment could be achieved through the senses, a tactic not acceptable to Methodism, or through the affections, which could only be reached by visits to each individual in his own home, there to discover his irritations, his anxieties and his needs. This the usual organisation of a chapel did not permit, and accordingly he pressed for a special Ministry to the Poor on the lines of the Boston Mission.

On Dr. Martineau's invitation, the sermons were repeated at the Paradise Street Chapel, and were followed by a meeting of the several congregations on Good Friday, April 1st, 1836, in the

---

[6] Thom, op. cit., p. 15.

[7] Inspired by Dr. Tuckerman, Missions had already been started in Bristol and Manchester.

[8] A survey had revealed that more than a third of the population were without religious affiliations.

Renshaw Street Chapel.[9]. After an opening service taken by Dr. Martineau, William Rathbone took the Chair, and the meeting proceeded with the formal constitution of the Domestic Mission. Moving with logical decorum through a series of propositions, beginning with the acceptance of their own obligation " to equalise . . . the moral condition of all His children ", the congregation agreed that " the existence in Liverpool of not fewer than 60,000 individuals who pass from childhood to age without any efficient means of religious culture, ought to excite the deepest sympathy on their behalf, and lead to active exertions for the improvement of their moral and social condition."[10]   Having further agreed that the existing church accommodation would be totally inadequate for this great number, though more than adequate for the number who at present wished to attend, they ultimately reached the proposal, made in two parts, that a Domestic Mission would be a means of effecting some improvement in this state of degeneration, and that the prospects for such a Mission justified the experiment. The final proposal was made by the Rev. Blanco White: " the appropriate duties of the Minister of the Poor shall be to establish an intercourse with a limited number of families of the neglected Poor—to put himself into close sympathy with their wants and feelings—to become to them a Christian adviser and friend—to promote the order and comfort of their homes, and the elevation of their social tastes—to bring them into a permanent connection with religious influences—and, above all, to promote an effective education of their children, and to shelter them from corrupting agencies."

There was apparently no suggestion at this stage that the benefits of the Mission would be in any sense mutual as between rich and poor, or even that voluntary service should be given by the supporters of the scheme: the obligation of the rich was simply to ensure that spiritual facilities in suitable form were provided for the poor. Though Dr. Tuckerman talked of his own Mission as "a Christian connexion between the rich and the poor, the virtuous and the vicious "[11] the rich were regarded as intrinsically unsuitable for the practical execution of the work, the gulf between visitor and visited being to them so plainly apparent that only a man of particular inspiration and talent could hope to bridge it.

William Rathbone was elected as first President, in which office he was subsequently succeeded by his son, the more eminent sixth William Rathbone, who attended this preliminary meeting as a boy of seventeen.[12]   Thomas Holt became Treasurer, and the

9 Eyre Evans, *op. cit.*, p. 12.
10 Holt, *op. cit.*, Chapter 2.
11 Holt, *op. cit.*, p. 11.
12 E. Rathbone, *op. cit.*, p. 70.

Committee included men of such important families as Bright, Gair, Yates and Roscoe.

The Unitarians were well aware of the difficult task they required of their Missioner, and his appointment was considered with great care. The Committee finally made a remarkable choice.

"We heard that there was a man living in the centre of Devonshire, of an ideal type, called by some a dreamer of dreams, but who simply belonged to that most genuine, that most productive form of the religious spirit, the practical mystic, with whom the trust in God, which we all profess, is simply so absolute that it is but a natural consequence that it should become the passion of his being to turn the visions of faith into the realities of life. We heard that he was one not mixing much with what is called the world, but a friend of the working man ever ready to throw himself, heart and soul, into every effort for the elevation of the people; not in the least what would be called a platform speaker, and yet one whose words, under emotion, of sympathy with right, or of protest against wrong, flowed in eloquent music or in fiery darts."[13]

This man was the Rev. John Johns, and it was evident from the first that he was of exceptional quality.

"I remember the first evening I spent with him after his settlement here with his family, but before he had ever seen the streets in which he was to find the future work of his life. He had not then much familiarity with the large towns, and he burned with impatience to be introduced to the localities which were henceforth to be the field of the world to him. He invited me to show him the district chosen for his first experiment, and I felt, as he walked through it, in earnest silence, searching out its worst places, gazing down into cellars and up into the lighted rooms, pausing long before the frequent buildings in which ardent spirits were sold, that solemn purposes were forming in his heart—and from that moment I could have no doubt that we had chosen rightly."[14]

The work Johns did was quiet and unostentatious. If it looks unenterprising to modern eyes, it is because of a failure to visualise it against its contemporary background of horrifying circumstances. His days were largely spent in visiting the homes of his poor neighbours whenever opportunity offered, of which visits he kept careful record, quoting them by way of illustration to his Reports. As and when opportunity occurred, small groups were gathered together and simple facilities for such activities as reading provided, on the principle which he evolved from his own experience, that "the most precious good that can be done for the poor is that which you can induce them to do for themselves."

[13] Speech by Rev. J. H. Thom at the Jubilee Meeting, 1st April, 1886.
[14] Rev. J. H. Thom, Sermon on the death of the Rev. John Johns, July 6th, 1847.

Gradually Johns made a secure place for himself in the district and with the supporting congregations of Unitarians. The Mission children were taken to Wombwell's Menagerie and congratulated on their behaviour by the proprietor's wife. His Assistant's wife cut out between ten and fifteen hundred yards of flannel into garments to be made up by the poor for their own use. A handsome gift of honey formed the basis of the manufacture of the Mission's own cough cure. The branch of the District Provident Society was one of the most successful in the town. When time permitted, Johns and his assistants were zealous in the collection of facts and information as to the customs and manners of the people, thus founding a tradition which make the long succession of Annual Reports invaluable historical sources, ranging as they do over the menace of the " huge piles of intellectual garbage in the shape of cheap periodicals ", the ramifications of the " Scotchman system " of pawning within pawning, the jealousy of the poor as opposed to the arrogance of the rich, the curious mimicry of social standards which deterred even the poorest from going to church inadequately dressed, and, most miraculously, the constant acceptance of fundamental human obligations even in the midst of apparently hopeless degradation.

Yet though the Reports make fascinating reading now there can be no denial of the fact that they have little to show in the way of results. This did not disturb Johns. In the face of the appalling gulf between what needed to be done, and what he alone could do, he maintained an enviable equanimity, based on the humble conviction that the value of his work lay not in what he achieved, but the proof he offered that achievement was actually possible. He believed that it was for lack of faith in the capacity for virtue in the poor that the rich allowed them to continue in their misery.

" Numbers have been, and are, passive spectators of the growth of social vice and misery, because they imagine that it is idle to think of arresting their course. Thus they lay for a time the spirit of holy misgiving; and thus, unchecked and despaired of, the evil grows and spreads in the dark cold shadow of faithlessness and neglect."[15]

The rousing of that spirit of holy misgiving in the rich Johns therefore regarded as the greatest service he could do for his poor neighbours: he was convinced that action must result if he could make others aware of the desperation of the poor in the hopelessness which threatened them, of their lack of any feeling of human warmth or sympathy, of their sense of exclusion from all that was good and lovely. With all the zeal of a missionary Johns wrote

[15] Annual Report, 1844.

into his Annual Reports picture after picture of the people amongst whom he now sojourned.

"Mothers, newly become such, without a garment on their persons, and with infants nearly as naked, lying upon straw or shavings, under a miserable covering, without fire or food, or the means of procuring them; children taken from their schools, in order to earn by begging, or by something but one degree above it, a few halfpence worth of bread for themselves and their parents; men in the prime of life, lounging at noonday across their beds, unable to procure work, and dependent upon the charity of their fellow-poor for subsistence; mothers of families only able to provide necessaries for their children, by pawning their little all, or by incurring debts wherever they could be trusted; persons in fevers, whose recovery was prevented and whose weakness was prolonged, by the want of all that promotes convalescence; and infirm and aged people, who were shivering out the last hours of life in absolute want of every thing that could sustain or endear it. . . ."[16]

Johns was well aware, however, that practical action as well as holy misgiving was required, and though he was clear that it was not the function of the Mission to campaign for specific reforms, he did not hesitate to point out to its sponsors the material improvements which were essential if the spiritual work was to flourish. The cellars must be shut up, was his constant cry, and his plea for the gradual extension of facilities for education to the whole population went so far as to visualise state responsibility. The condition of the slums, which the supporters of the Mission had hoped might have improved as an indirect result of the strengthening of moral fibre, Johns quickly realised was in fact the actual cause of much degeneration, the only remedy being action by the rich and powerful. Indeed, he went further, and declared that unless material conditions were remedied, not only would social virtue still decline, but life itself might be endangered, a statement greeted with considerable disbelief.[17]

"I have often found their physical wants so great, as not merely to embitter life, but to antedate its close. I have no hesitation in saying, that an unsuspected amount of human existence must annually be sacrificed, in this and similar towns, *from simple and absolute starvation*. No jury sits on these neglected remains; no horror-stricken neighbourhood is electrified by the rumour, that one has died among them of cold, and nakedness, and hunger. Obscurity clouds the death-bed; and oblivion rests upon the grave. But, unknown as it may be to the world at large, the fact is awfully

[16] Annual Report, 1837.

[17] For example, see *The Liverpool Night Asylum for the Homeless Poor, 1839*, in which Egerton Smith, the founder of the Asylum, describes the incredulity which greeted his exposure of conditions amongst the poor.

certain,—that not a few of our poor, especially of the aged and infirm, die, winter after winter, of no disease but inanition."[18]

Though they respected Johns's work, this emphasis on the need for drastic social reforms was not the result the founders of the Mission had hoped for from their experiment. They had cherished the belief that, given spiritual aid, the extreme burden of poverty could be alleviated by the efforts of the poor man himself, and that so far as they personally were concerned, their duty to the poor had been done when they authorised Johns to act as spiritual almoner on their behalf. The necessity for a programme of social reform as a basis for this was difficult to accept by people who had not themselves penetrated to the homes of the people, but to add to the difficulty Johns made it plain that even more was required of them. Not more in the material sense, for though he was constantly pestered for alms, so much so that he had sometimes to retreat from a court till the turmoil subsided, Johns remained of the firm conviction that even if he had had a larger Poor Purse, relief was only to be given as an emergency measure. Benevolent societies and relief schemes he roundly denounced[19] as generally doing more harm than good. Instead, the Mission Reports voice appeal after appeal for more helpers from the ranks of the better-off, while Johns and his successors harped constantly on the fundamental need of the poor for sympathy and guidance.

"None but those who have mingled with the poor can form any idea, either of the sullen discontent generated in their too suspicious minds, by the impression that they are neglected and uncared for by their more fortunate fellow creatures, or of the brightness and joy which the occasional visit, so that it be made with delicacy and respect, of a sympathising friend from the wealthier classes casts athwart their gloomy hearths."[20]

In practice this was an extremely difficult relationship to achieve when the whole trend of thought and custom was towards the separation of society into classes. Johns was outstanding in that he was not only willing but positively eager to accept the fact of his common humanity with the most desperate and degenerate of characters. Writing of his first few months in Liverpool, he said: —

"Within those months, I have seen, what, had I *not* seen it, I could not have imagined. I have seen life under forms which took from it all that, in my eyes, made it happy, hopeful, or even human. I have seen life under forms, which it made it necessary for me to rouse up all the strength of my previous reasonings and convictions, in order to convince myself that these were really fellow-beings."[21]

[18] Annual Report, 1837.
[19] See p. 32.
[20] Annual Report, 1850.
[21] Annual Report, 1837.

The magnificence of his short life was that neither this experience nor any in the years that followed diminished his faith in the essential humanity of even the lowest. He was actually able to turn to his own ends the tide of degeneration which swept over his people during the last few years of his life, humbly claiming of that bitter experience that "distress on the one side and sympathy on the other, have opened heart to heart till all strangership was done away".[22] That the essence of charity lay in the opening of heart unto human heart was, however, a lesson too difficult for belief by those who had not shared his experience and Johns roused in his hearers only a deep misgiving.

In this mixed mood of doubt and disappointment the supporters of the Mission were called upon to face the fearful realities of the Hungry Forties.

It was by now accepted that conditions in Liverpool were worse than almost anywhere else in the country, and it is beyond imagination to grasp what it must have meant to the already overcrowded and under-employed working classes to find themselves swamped by the flood of what appeared to be half-savage Irish immigrants of the winter of 1846, and the following spring. The previous confusion was as nothing to the chaos into which the town was now plunged; if the problems of poverty had tended to breed defeatism before, they went far beyond it to the point of menace now. As always, housing proved the bottleneck. The Medical Officer of Health's calm estimate of the position in his very first Annual Report is as fearful as any more lurid description:—

"The 1st of January, 1847, found this pauper immigration steadily increasing, and it continued in such rapidly progressive rates, that by the end of June not less than 300,000 Irish had landed in Liverpool. Of these it was very moderately estimated that from 60,000 to 80,000 had located themselves amongst us, occupying every nook and cranny of the already overcrowded lodging-houses, and forcing their way into cellars (about 3,000 in number) which had been closed under the provisions of the Health Act, 1842. In different parts of Liverpool 50 or 60 of these destitute people were found in a house containing three or four small rooms, about 12 feet by 10; and in more than one instance upwards of 40 were found sleeping in a cellar."[23]

Housing conditions in the nineteenth century have often been described, so no more need be said of them here than will convey the particular horror of the situation as it developed in Liverpool. Dr. Duncan, who was for ten years attached to the Liverpool Dispensaries before his appointment in 1846 as the first Medical Officer

[22] Annual Report, 1847
[23] Frazer, *op. cit.*, p. 57.

of Health in the country, estimated that half of the total working-class population of 175,000 were then living in courts, and that of these some thirty to forty thousand occupied upwards of eight thousand cellars. Some of Dr. Duncan's figures, which he quoted in a lecture to the Literary and Philosophical Society in 1843 read now like printer's errors. He knew of one court which gave a return of one person per square yard, and of another area which worked out at the rate of over six hundred thousand per square mile; " even these figures of over-crowding, terrible as they are, do not quite plumb the depths of misery and degradation in which the casual labourers of Liverpool and their families had to live at that period ".[24] Dr. Duncan wrote that he found it impossible to describe the state of many of the entries and passages in the most densely peopled streets, contenting himself with the tart observation that " it is sufficient to say that they require the most careful management of both eye and nose on the part of the unpractised visitor ".[25] Yet so loathsome were the scenes about him that he felt compelled to call attention to their existence. Talking of cellar dwellings he says : —

" On one occasion I had to grope my way (at noon-day) into a house in a court in Thomas Street; and on a candle being lighted, I discovered my patient lying on a heap of straw in one corner, while in the opposite corner of the room a donkey was comfortably established, and immediately under the window was the dunghill which the donkey was employed to assist in gathering from the street."[26]

Johns, who had previously thought that he could discern signs of slight improvement in social conditions, now found himself baffled by the difficulty of merely making credible the incredible conditions he daily witnessed. His Annual Reports overflow with his compassion for the struggles of those about him to maintain not only some shred of human decency but life itself.

" The last time I was in Brick Street, the effluvia were scarcely supportable. I have often to return from those places with a sick stomach, and an aching head. If such be the effect upon an occasional visitor, can it be innoxious to those who are exposed to it night and day?"[27]

The court houses, which even in their original conception had been villainous enough, were now crowded to suffocation, sub-let room by room and even part-room by part-room. The cellars

[24] *Ibid*, p. 27.

[25] *The Sanitary Condition of the Labouring Population of England*, 1842, *Local Reports*: p. 287.

[26] *Ibid.*, p. 287.

[27] Annual Report, 1845.

became abominable beyond belief, graves for the dying rather than
abodes for the living.

". . . houses of the lowest class were so crowded during this
period, that it was a common thing to find every apartment of
the dwelling occupied by several families. No curtain, no parti-
tion exists; no separation of any kind can, in most of these cases,
be practicable. The father, mother and children of one family
sleep together in one corner; the father, mother and children of
another family sleep together in another; ditto, ditto, ditto, in a
third, etc. Sometimes there were beds upon stocks, but I have
latterly seen more of cases, in which the litters (for I can call them
nothing else) are spread upon the floor or pavement, perhaps without any article of furniture in the apartment, or at most a broken
chair or two, a log of wood, or a stool."[28]

Finally and inevitably, cholera broke out, and every thought
was bent upon living through the immediate crisis, and helping
others to do the same. Futile now to think of charity in terms of
visiting the poor to stimulate them to self-improvement. Where the
bare necessities of life were lacking, and disease threatened the
starving, it was bread alone which was required of the rich man by
the poor.

"The waves of ordinary suffering swelled at once into billows;
and day after day, and week after week, they rolled and rolled upon
us, with the same tumult of wild expectancy, till the heart of pity
was sick, and the hand of relief was weary. Day after day, and
week after week, the same crowds of applicants besieged the door
of your office lobby; stairs, landing-place, and even the street
outside, were thronged with eager and pallid faces, wearing every
shade and variety of expression that misery can produce, or hypo-
crisy feign. Every tide floated in a new importation of Irish misery,
and the snow was loosened from our doors by hordes of bare-footed
beggars."[29]

Johns's tenth and last Report which covers the bitter winter and
spring of 1846 and 1847 is a magnificent piece of descriptive
writing, overflowing with that compassionate sensibility which
earned for him the description of being as sensitive as if he had no
skin. Such depth of pity combined with such steadfastness of gaze
in the face of circumstances so dark must be rare in the annals of
human experience. By chance, he wrote on the death that year of
two of the Mission's founder members, Mr. Gair and Mr. Holt,
what was to be quoted as his own epitaph so shortly afterwards:
"Let us never forget that such men were, nor live as if we had forgotten their beautiful lives". The following year he died of the
cholera caught in the course of visiting the sick in his district.

[28] Annual Report, 1847.
[29] Annual Report, 1847.

D

Johns's death profoundly shocked the congregation who had inaugurated the Mission for they felt that he had died in doing what they themselves should have done. The words they put upon his tombstone show that they fully appreciated the significance of his personal example: —

> " Born a poet and having his natural delight in a Poet's
> contemplation of the Works of God, he left the retired
> Ministry that seemed most congenial to him amid
> the calm beauty of his native Devon, and
> became the Friend and daily Companion
> of the Poor in crowded woe-worn
> streets, there to draw forth the holier
> beauty of man's spiritual nature in conditions
> of severest trial, and to find for himself a more
> real communion with God in the faith, patience
> and penitence of the most afflicted of his children.
> He lived in the spirit of his great office and died its
> sacrifice. In a time of pestilence the Death Angel met him
> across the bodies of the stricken
> whom he was tending with his own hands."[30]

Johns had made his point; he could depart in peace. But he left to the sponsors of the Mission a legacy of uneasy mind and troubled conscience. Though they did not deny the value of his work they were depressed by their feeling that he had failed to discover a solution to the problem of poverty, or to disperse their sense of responsibility for the moral and material condition of the poor. To them, the lesson of his experience was simply that little in the way of moral improvement could be expected of the working classes until the crushing weight upon their spirits of the physical burden of poverty was eased. Their own lives were conducted in the faith that material and moral welfare were inseparables: it went against the grain to admit that spiritual improvement must wait upon a drive for better sanitation.

This interpretation of Johns's experience was based on a misapprehension of his conception of charity. Johns had always assumed that the provision of a minimum of " physical civilisation " was the natural responsibility of society as a whole and the particular obligation of the rich: his personal contribution was to prove that the present degeneration of the poor was due to the lack of this minimum rather than to their inferior moral quality. What he failed to add, so sweetly did his own love for the poor become him, was that the fulfilment of this obligation by the rich was only a necessary condition of true charity and not charity itself. This distinction the sponsors of the Mission failed to grasp. Much as they respected

[30] Annual Report, 1884.

the manner of Johns's life and even more of his death, they found it hard to understand the practical implications of his high estimate of the importance of the relationship between one human being and another.   That warmth of sympathy, that opening of heart unto heart which supported him in his depressing and difficult task, and which he regarded as the real charity of man to his brother, was left an unexplained mystery to the people on whose behalf he had taken up work as a Missioner.

Reluctantly they abandoned their dreams of virtue triumphant over all, and turned their attention to the hard facts of housing and sanitation.   As a Report on the Mission's work shortly after the death of John's sadly declared, hope for the future seemed rather to lie in " a great work of physical civilisation . . . First, that which is natural; afterward, that which is spiritual ".[31]

[31] Annual Report, 1850.

CHAPTER IV

THE CHALLENGE OF THE NEW POOR: (ii) " PHYSICAL CIVILISATION ",
1850-1870

As the shouting and the turmoil of the 'forties receded into history, the epidemic proportions of fever and famine subsided to what, by contrast, presented an appearance of normality. It was now taken for granted that social conditions should be related to the needs of industry rather than of agriculture, of the town rather than the country. The Municipal Corporations Act of 1835, the Health of Towns campaign, the long series of legislative acts covering the poor law, education, and the public services generally, are evidence of the effort to provide the new towns with public services and amenities specifically planned to meet the requirements of an industrial community. With this went the realisation that the new poverty was no passing problem but a permanent feature of urban life whose remedy called for a drastic alteration in the nature of charitable effort. Dr. Duncan was one of the first to state publicly his opinion[1] that the wretchedness of the poor was the inevitable consequence of their circumstances and not necessarily their own fault, but he was by no means alone in taking this view. There was, for instance, a growing belief that the principle of the harsh treatment of the poor which, under the inspiration of Bentham had resulted in the Poor Law of 1834, was not applicable to the helpless inhabitants of an industrial slum. The attitude of religion towards the poor reflected a similar trend, if the words of the Bishop of Chester to the Association for the Promotion of Social Science in Liverpool in 1858, may be taken as typical. He assumed, and there is no evidence that his hearers disagreed with him, that religious principles could not be applied to the monotonous and mechanical tasks which composed the life of the working man, although he could nevertheless " be acting on a real principle of religious obedience, if, regarding the necessities and duties of his lot as the will and appointment of God, he earns his daily bread with a contented mind, and shares it amongst his family with a grateful heart ".[2] The formation of the Association for the Promotion of Social Science was significant of the change in public opinion, indicating a new approach to poverty as a problem capable of intellectual rather than moral solution.

This change was possibly the most important legacy of the previous unhappy decade. The District Provident Society had long ago

[1] *The Sanitary Condition of the Labouring Population of England*, 1842. *Local Reports.*

[2] *Proceedings*, p. 1.

46

commented[3] on the difficulty of preaching to men with empty bellies, but the climate of the times had discouraged it from going on to draw the obvious conclusion. The circumstances were now very different.

Life in the town no longer resembled that in a rural community. A considerable proportion of rich and poor alike were of the second and third generations and had never lived in an ordered community where rights and duties were integrated by tradition into a body of social custom and habit. This fact alone would have constituted a considerable problem in social re-education, but to it was added the complication of profound changes in the social structure. The obliteration of the old distinction between the poor and the working classes was common to the whole nation, but in Liverpool it was emphasised by local peculiarities to such a degree as to make it virtually impossible to maintain the traditional distinction between those who earned their living and those who deserved the benefits of charity. The emergence of the middle classes which also characterised the period, was similarly exaggerated by local circumstances. The consequent clear-cut opposition of class to class, and the necessity for working out satisfactory relations between the two groups as classes and not as individuals, was to underlie charitable effort for the rest of the century.

The poverty of the heritage of the city poor was almost beyond belief. Such preparation for life as the children received they picked up mainly on the streets, and their lack of training in moral and social habits was made apparent by the fact that " crime, and more particularly juvenile crime, is fearfully on the increase ".[4] Overcrowding, the word a mere label for a whole complex of miseries, had become an accepted condition: the Domestic Missioner, for instance, knew of not one house in his whole district which was in the occupation of a single family.[5] Premises hurriedly erected or made over to meet the housing emergency of earlier years, were by now settling into a state of chronic decay, " gloomy, battered, tottering, mouldy and mutilated ";[6] and already the poorer parts of the town were characterized by the often deplored " blinding stench ",[7] which was as much that of accumulated age as of present filth. Though valiant efforts were made by individuals to retain their self-respect, the general pressure of conditions enforced a constant levelling down of social standards. Against this, their status in

[3] See p. 30.

[4] *Liverpool Life: its Pleasures, Practices and Pastimes.* (Reprinted from the *Liverpool Mercury*, 1857). 2nd Series. p. 38.

[5] Domestic Mission. Annual Report, 1857.

[6] *The Courts and Alleys of Liverpool.* Described from personal inspection by Hugh Shimmin (1864).

[7] *Ibid.*

industry as mere hands, and the belief that the working classes
existed literally to work, provided no defence, and the only means
of escape was alcohol. Drunkenness gained a grip upon the community which rivalled even the horrible housing conditions in its
capacity to breed degeneration: its universality is a measure of the
depth of misery to which the labouring classes were reduced.

Worst of all, even the poor themselves had come to accept their
own poverty. The bitter rebellion of Chartism against the whole
concept of industrialism had declined into a struggle to mark out the
labourer's rights within the existing framework, whilst the outburst
of miscellaneous alms and soup giving which marked the particularly
cruel spring of 1855 served to confirm in the minds of the poor the
lesson of the plague years that it was possible to live without working, so that poverty gained status as an accepted way of life, with its
own conception of its rights. The indifference of the individual poor
to ambition or even creature comfort was one of the most baffling
problems ever encountered by the Victorian philanthropist.

Little trace remained of the early interest of the working classes
in such schemes for adult education as Mechanics Institutes and
Mutual Improvement Societies which had shown promise of
developing into self-governing associations. For this, the exhaustion
resulting from long working hours, the general debasement of the
use of leisure which accompanied the influx of labour of the 'forties,
and the resentment of that patronage which seemed inevitably to
accompany the necessary financial assistance from the upper
classes, was responsible. Nevertheless, the numerous Burial Clubs,
Friendly Societies and other groups are evidence of the efforts of the
poor to fashion a society of their own. Why, with all their appreciation of the virtues of self-respect and independence, the Victorian
philanthropist should have failed to recognise the potentialities of
such spontaneous groups as training grounds in self-help will be
discussed later in this chapter.

The only agencies which made any attempt to build up a sense
of community were the religious bodies, though the street was often
the only space which the preacher could call his own in those
crowded districts. The Rev. H. Postance has described how in 1856,
he was appointed to a Parish containing 500 Protestant families and
412 Roman Catholic families, " lying as a kind of sediment along
the edge of the Queen's and Brunswick Docks. There were at this
time, more than 300 families without Bibles and 900 adult persons
confessed that they attended no place of worship whatever. The
district was so closely built up that no site could then be found for
a Church, and for two years I was obliged to preach in the open
air, whenever the weather permitted . . . at times I have had rough
handling as a Street Preacher, having been stoned on one occasion
in Worthington Street, in which we had at the time only three

Protestant families; almost the whole of the inhabitants were living like heathens, the majority of the male portion being night-soil men . . . . The locality was indeed waxing worse and worse, and the Dissenters, who were unable to proceed on the voluntary principle in such a locality as this, began to seek fresh sites for their Chapels, three of them having been deserted in a comparatively short time ".[8] Starting thus from nothing, he began the long task of providing his church with such facilities as National Schools and Mission Halls essential to its work as a social agency. To obtain and clear a site by the demolition of houses, to raise by begging from the wealthy the necessary money (one or other of his patrons usually included with his donation a silver trowel with which to lay the foundation stone and a personal cheque to eke out the official stipend of £150), to clear the brothels from the doorstep of his Schools, to restrain a rowdy theatre from disturbing his Sunday services, to raise an endowment fund in order to gain permission to abandon the system of pew rents, this was the typical pattern of church work among the poor, though not all were as zealous as Mr. Postance.

Against this picture of habitual misery must be set the increasing comfort and prosperity of the middle classes, a contrast emphasised by the physical separation of the population into suburb and slum. The middle classes, whose numbers were increasing rapidly, were finding that improved facilities for transport, such as buses and trains, as well as boats across the river, made it possible for lesser men to ape the style of living adopted by the merchant princes, and middle class suburbs were rapidly being built.

Yet though the phrase " two worlds "[9] is commonly applied to the resulting society, the middle classes were in fact far from constituting a single group. The tone was set by the aristocracy, who consisted primarily of the old corporate or governing families.[10] To them had been added families who had come to the town about the turn of the century, and by their commercial success and sense of civic responsibility had assumed positions of leadership in local affairs, amongst whom the Unitarian families of Rathbone and Holt were outstanding. The influence of this aristocracy, itself no coherent group, was quite out of proportion to their numbers or wealth. Their financial stability and the continuity provided by even three or four generations, enabled them to exercise a marked influence on local affairs. However, as the town filled up, they tended to conduct

[8] *The Difficulties of Pastoral and Educational Work in Poor Parishes.* A paper read before the Liverpool Clerical Society at St. George's Hall by the Rev. H. Postance, October 6th, 1884.

[9] Disraeli coined the phrase in 1845.

[10] *Liverpool a Few Years Since.* By an Old Stager. (James Aspinall, himself a member of one such Corporate family.) (Holden, 1885.)

their affairs in an exclusion which centred in the first place upon family and secondly upon membership of a particular church or chapel. This added to their charms in the eyes of social climbers, but eventually resulted in a loss of warmth in their social contacts which was to undermine their best endeavours. A typical merchant was described as ranking

". . . with the Brights, Parkers, Branckers, Mosses and Hornbys of this generation. Although his business placed him in contact with upstart money-seekers, if among them he was not of them, for he had been born to a high commercial position, and been educated at a university; had from youth upward nourished his personal piety among intelligent Christians of cultural minds and refined manners, and thus was separated by a wide gulf from the seething crowd of those who had no grandfathers, and who, whatever their energetic ambition might aspire to in the future, had no past which they cared to talk about."[11]

Following on the heels of this local aristocracy of merchant princes, whose stability was their outstanding feature, came a motley crowd of newcomers, jostling for position, subject to rapid fluctuations of fortune which might in equal probability carry them into high society in London or the counties or eliminate them altogether from the social scene. But the real bulk of the middle classes was provided by the huge class of " black-coated " workers. It was estimated that there were in Liverpool by 1871 seventeen thousand clerks working in the centre of the city alone.[12] These were in addition to the merchants, tradesmen and professional men whose numbers can only be guessed at.

All of these, as they withdrew before the invasion of immigrant labour, sorted themselves out according to their status and their means. Those who could afford most, went furthest afield, where they built themselves country houses : those of lesser means, moved lesser distances, where they put up the best appearance they could by developing suburbs in pseudo country house style. A journey through what are now the inner suburbs of the city reveals the social consequences, namely, special quarters for the rich, for those of middling fortune, and for the poor.[13]

Between these, there was little intercourse.

"There was no cordiality between various large sections of Liverpool clerks and their employees. There is scarcely a pretence of friendliness. . . There are firms still whose partners invite their clerks to dinner once a year, and who give Christmas boxes, or make welcome presents when babies come to increase their humble

[11] B. G. Orchard, *Twenty Literary Portraits of Business Men* (Matthews Bros., 1884), p. 82.
[12] B. G. Orchard, *The Clerks of Liverpool*, 1871.
[13] Ramsay Muir, *History of Liverpool* (Williams and Norgate, 1907), p. 304.

friends' expenses. Nevertheless, it is unfortunately true that, taken altogether the masters are hard and their tender mercies cruel."[14]

The physical disintegration of the town into suburbs on a basis of social distinction was, in fact, a demonstration of the extent to which the disintegration of society, inherited from the nineteenth century, had been magnified by the stresses of the boom period. It was accompanied inevitably, by an indifference to each others' affairs which reached its most astonishing heights as between the poor and the community at large. With the exception of the small group of socially conscientious, of whom the Unitarians were notable examples, the bulk of the town did not assume any interest in or responsibility for the condition of the poor or their relief.

"Now the dock is far away from the counting-house, and its duties are left to others. The merchant is employed all day in the direction of transactions; the executive details are left to subordinates. His work done, the merchant, and even the large shopkeeper, leaves it for his residence at a distance in the country, in a suburb of the overgrown town, or at the West-end of London. . . . His wife and daughters can no longer call upon the labourer's sick or troubled family in the short walk which formerly brought them into the country. If such a visit has to be paid the carriage must be ordered and time spared for a drive of five or six miles into or through the town . . . the less leisure, intenser work, or more luxurious life of the present generation will complete the estrangement of the rich from the poor."[15]

Evidence of this indifference was provided in 1854 when the Rev. A. Hume analysed the lists of subscribers to various Liverpool charities.[16] He found that the bulk of the money subscribed to the principal local charities under consideration came from a handful of people; about half of the total amount was given by less than 700 subscribers out of a total list of 9,760. Judging by the poor rate list, he estimated that a further 30,000 heads of families could well afford to contribute and he made various suggestions by which this might be achieved, such as the spreading of interest by collecting a larger number of small subscriptions, and the publication of a joint list in order to shame into activity those who gave no practical support to local charities. The survey was the subject of a paper read to the local Historical Society, and evidently aroused interest, or at least curiosity, for at a subsequent meeting at which a paper on the manufacture of cobalt was read, Dr. Hume's lists were exhibited, along

[14] B. G. Orchard, *op. cit.*

[15] William Rathbone, *Social Duties,* By a Man of Business (Macmillan and Co., 1867), p. 9.

[16] Rev. A. Hume, D.C.L., LL.D. *Analysis of the Subscribers to the Various Liverpool Charities.* Transactions of the Historic Society of Lancashire and Cheshire, vol. vii, 1854-55.

with a set of Wedgwood's cameos systematically arranged. This paper could only fill with despondency those who took the view that the exercise of charity was as essential to the moral welfare of the prosperous as gratitude and fortitude were to the impoverished.

It must nevertheless be acknowledged that to bridge the gulf in person, to go and see for oneself what conditions were like, would have been a strange idea for any ordinary citizen to entertain. The slums must have been a dim reality to the inhabitants of the suburbs, whose gaze was in any case fixed rather on those above than those below them in the social scale. " Scotland Ward is perhaps less fragrant than Abercromby. You will not find there many nursery maids reading novels while the infants under their charge, in muslin slips and pink waist belts, are chasing each other round the well-kept gardens of a handsome square. The atmosphere is not so bright: no graceful carriages with ' ladyes fayre ' drive from door to door; no footmen in scarlet and gold thunder with quintuple ran-tans at lofty portals; and the scavengers eschew, if they can, that distant region ".[17] It must have seemed a far cry from such surroundings to those Dr. Duncan described where only the priest and the doctor might safely venture, and the youngest daughter of a missionary curate on her way to Sunday School was liable to have two of her teeth knocked out by street ruffians.[18]

Yet though the middle classes might long remain indifferent to the misery of the poor, never again could they claim to be unaware of their existence. The cholera epidemic of the late 'forties had dramatically demonstrated to them the danger to the whole social fabric of the presence in their midst of a " . . . people swayed by no inward sympathy with the purpose of God, swept by passion, tortured by want, dark at soul, held back from headlong impulse only by those habits of submission which, at ordinary times, keep the most powerful animals in obedience to man, but which break, like rotten reins, when the fierce nature strains against them ".[19]

For the first time, the middle classes began to realise the implications of the gulf between their own material standards of living and those of the poor, and the even more startling gulf between their own moral standards and those of the poor. They deplored the hostility with which they and their way of life were regarded by the lowest classes: the irritation of the poor against God and man profoundly shocked them. Indeed, the impression is unavoidable that they were more alarmed by the degeneration of the poor than moved by compassion for their unhappy state. The accepted faith in the philosophy of self-help denied the necessity for anyone to

[17] *Pen and Ink Sketches of Liverpool Town Councillors*, by a local Artist (Reprinted from the *Liverpool Mercury*, 1857), p. 105.
[18] *Porcupine*, 25th November, 1865.
[19] Thom, *op. cit.* p. 176.

remain poor who was willing to live industriously and virtuously, and on those grounds the middle classes felt justified in refusing to help those who failed to help themselves. But the lack of desire in the poor for such a life, and the all-too evident preference for quite another sort of behaviour, could not be so easily dismissed. This was particularly apparent in regard to the use of leisure. So far as work was concerned, there was, in theory at least, no reason why the man should not by industry and thrift become the master, but in their leisure-time it was obvious that an ominous distinction existed between the two. Public attention fastened on the behaviour of the poor outside their working hours, and the tentative movement for providing facilities for rational recreation for the people received unexpected support. The provision of improving entertainment for the masses, and of free public lectures on topics of behaviour became a recognised form of charitable work.[20] This interest in the recreations of the poor encouraged the *Liverpool Mercury* to publish in 1856 an article by a free-lance journalist named Hugh Shimmin, describing in open language a " working-class saturnalia " which he had witnessed on Bidston Hill. This proved so exactly to the public taste that Shimmin proceeded to visit and describe the whole gamut of low life as displayed in the local concert saloons, dance halls, amusement arcades and other commercially-inspired facilities for the use of leisure, including horse-racing at Aintree. This lively demonstration of the decay in social standards, which revealed the supposedly self-respecting artisan to be in actual fact nothing more than a lounger living solely for low pleasure, came as a shock and surprise to the general public, all the more so because it was incidentally made plain that gentlemen were also prone to indulge in such amusements. It was said of the articles when they reappeared in book form the following year[21] that they " revealed to the people of Liverpool an abyss of sin, dark and dreadful, of the depths of which many of them had but a vague conception ".[22] And it is evident that by endowing this abyss with reality Shimmin succeeded where all the jeremiads of the philanthropic had failed, in rousing the middle classes to the dangers of the situation.

The remarkable local success of *Liverpool Life* brought the struggling campaign against the dancing saloons to a triumphant conclusion. More sketches followed, then public lectures, and finally, in 1860, inspired by a visit of the Savage Club, the founding of *The Porcupine* itself, a satirical and miscellaneous weekly journal. This shortly came under Shimmin's sole editorship, and

[20] See, for example, W. S. Cain, *Hugh Stowell Brown* (Routledge & Sons, 1888).

[21] Under the title of *Liverpool Life*.

[22] *A Commentary on " Liverpool Life ".* Reprint of a lecture by the Rev. Hugh Stowell Brown (no date).

proved so well-suited to his purpose that it was by that name rather than his own that he came to be pointed out as an outstanding character about the town.

Week by week for almost twenty years, until his death in 1879, *Porcupine* pilloried in biting, racy prose the smug, the patronising, the mean, the hypocrite, regardless of whether he found his victim amongst the richest of old families or the most wretched of the poor. Indeed, it was one of his greatest charms for the climbing middle classes that he " had a provokingly quick eye for the faults of his own party, and a puckish delight in placing these in odious and ridiculous light "[23] which frequently resulted in the public embarrassment of leading men. But the satire and the rough wit were inspired by a passionate conviction that the improvement of the condition of the poor was a public responsiblity which it was his purpose to shock the better-off into accepting. This by vigorous and provocative exhortation, by rude indifference to the feelings of individuals, by remorseless attack upon bodies public and private, he succeeded in doing to a remarkable extent, as much by his infinite care in collecting his facts as by his recklessness in delivering the subsequent blow. And when, as was bound to happen, this resulted in a libel suit which saw him in gaol as a bankrupt, so widespread was the admiration for his integrity that he was housed in the Chaplain's own comfortable room whilst a public subscription was raised to meet the expenses of the action.

His personal pursuit of the facts as to housing rightly earned him a reputation as a sanitary expert. The series of articles in *Porcupine* in 1864 on *The Courts and Alleys of Liverpool* was based on personal visits to practically every house in every court in a certain area about Paradise Street. Culminating in the grim description of a " Dark Episode in Little Hell ", these articles were reprinted as part of the campaign for Parliamentary powers enabling the Corporation to mitigate the evils he there described and won for Shimmin the warm appreciation of the Borough Surveyor and his medical colleagues.

Yet humanitarian though he openly declared his purpose to be, Shimmin bore no resemblance to the merchant prince of exclusive philanthropic circles. He was born of working class parents in the Isle of Man, received such formal education as the Manesty Lane School could provide, was apprenticed to the book-binding trade, and filled in the gaps in his education by membership of the Mutual Improvement Society attached to the Liverpool Institute. A shining example of the successfully self-educated man, he took some pride in concealing the fact behind a carefully cultivated provincial brusquerie. His intellectual attainments apart,

[23] *Liverpool Daily Post*, 13th January, 1879.

Shimmin was typical of the class to which he belonged. His charity, like theirs, sprang from a personal experience of poverty.[24] From it, the responsible patronage of traditional benevolence was excluded by that feeling of being personally involved in the condition of the poor which was to prove such an important factor in the charitable relationship. His lapses into sentimentality, which accord so strangely with the practical approach of the housing expert, are explicable only as theirs were, in terms of the lack of established principles and practice which was inevitable in so newly formed a social class. The uncontrolled emotionalism which, carried to excess eventually brought about his death from a " tendency of blood to the head "[25] was as characteristic of them as it was of him.

Charity had indeed secured an unexpected ally in Hugh Shimmin, but one who was received with mixed feelings. It is significant that his services were more highly valued in public health than in charitable circles. True, the Chaplain of the Borough Gaol and Mr. Rathbone openly supported the publication of *Liverpool Life* with commendatory letters, Mr. Rathbone adding as a further application of Shimmin's principle that publicity is the true cure of social evil the suggestion that gin palaces should be compelled to extend their plate glass windows to the ground in order to expose to public censure the scenes within. But on the whole the established philanthropists of the town made little use of him, for his capacity to shock offended them as much, if in a different way, as it did the new middle classes of which he was himself a member. They failed to realise that they had in Shimmin the very interpreter of charitable principle for lack of whom they found themselves unable to prevent the new sentiment in favour of the poor from running riot.

And run riot it certainly did. Shimmin had set out to shock the public into action, but he was quite unable to deal with the response which his efforts provoked. Compounded of a mingled sense of bafflement, irritation and guilt, the new interest in the poor was as different from that of the traditional philanthropist as the new poverty itself was from the old. It was their failure to realise this which deprived the established philanthropists of much of their influence, and it was on this rock that charitable theory and practice were eventually to split. The gulf between " old families " and the new middle class was in many ways as wide as that separating rich from poor. As a result, those who might have been expected to direct middle class charity into profitable channels found that often they were only able to inspire a snobbish imitation of their own

[24] He enjoyed the joke that he had begun life as a wave, his first money being earned as a lad in a penny theatre in the poorer part of the town, dancing under a sheet which was supposed to represent the ocean.

[25] *Liverpool Daily Post*, 13th January, 1879.

philanthropy from which the underlying integrity of purpose was sadly lacking. The public quickly realised that charitable activity afforded admirable opportunities for overcoming the barrier of exclusiveness with which the local aristocracy had surrounded themselves, and participation in charitable schemes even began to replace church membership as a means of effecting desirable social contacts. Thus inspired, philanthropy became a mere matter of fashion.

"The most fashionable amusement of the present age is philanthropy. Liverpool which delights in following a fashion of any kind, pants and puffs to keep well up with this in especial. But it is a fashion, and we would not have the working-man suppose that all the gentlemen and ladies of Liverpool, who now evince so keen a solicitude for his welfare, really do care quite as much about him or understand his condition and his wants quite as well as they give out. No small number of these benevolent persons are philanthropic because it is the fashion to be so; because it brings them into passing contact with this Bishop or that Earl, or even with Mr. Cropper or Mr. Rathbone, or any other of our leading local philanthropists. Not a few ladies, who will visit the garret of a working-man's wife, and talk in the most condescending way, and put on the most friendly interest in the progress of the children, would quiver to the outermost hoops of their crinolines if asked to sit down to tea with the wife of a grocer. We know of a Liverpool philanthropist who will lecture night after night to working-men, and will grasp their hands all round, and who would nevertheless sooner perish than offer his precious fingers to the governess when he visits a friend's family. Because, to shake hands with the working-man, to talk with the working-man's wife, only elevates you, don't you see—makes you a patron and a condescending magnate, and all that—but the grocer's wife or the governess, why, creatures of that class might be putting themselves on an equality. . . ."[26]

The second meeting of the National Association for the Promotion of Social Science, held in the newly built St. George's Hall in 1858, had an astonishing success in view of its sober intention of providing a factual basis upon which to plan remedial action. What had been organised as a serious attempt to apply scientific methods to social problems developed into a particularly attractive form of social activity. *Porcupine* wrote bitterly of social science as the easiest and most respectable of all the varieties of philanthropy.

"Take up Social Science as nineteen-twentieths of our Liverpool folk do, as something which makes a shopkeeper for a moment hail-fellow with a lord, and flatters an alderman into believing himself a philosopher. . . . Are you a Liverpool trader? Bring

[26] *Porcupine,* 1st June, 1861.

your wife and daughters to the meetings, and be sure you are seen shaking hands with Theodore Rathbone. . . . Once the philanthropist had heavy work, loathsome tasks, public contempt; now he has light and pleasant labour, fashionable honours, the praises of lords, the puffing of newspapers. . . ."[27]

To explain why " social science " should have seized the popular imagination at this particular moment would involve a major analysis of Victorian town life. There was, for instance, the need of the middle classes for some interest, respectable but not too high-brow and preferably scientific, to occupy the leisure-time many of them were enjoying for the first time, leisure for the cultivation of which their peasant ancestry had not prepared them, and for which they lacked the cultural equipment of the educated merchant classes. There was the universal enthusiasm for the novelty of watching the wheels of democracy go round, for which the committees, conferences and annual meetings of charitable associations provided ample opportunity. There was, too, the satisfaction to be derived by those whose own social position was a matter for constant care, from the exercise of a patronage previously the prerogative of the ruling classes. And there was the opportunity for discussing subjects which under conditions of contemporary prudery, had acquired all the fascination of the forbidden.

On the other hand, there was, especially amongst women, a doubtless unsuspected dissatisfaction with urban life, an unrecognised need to serve, and so to become part of, an ordered and stable community. Nor can the suspicion be avoided that underneath everything else lay a common compunction at the price exacted from the working classes by the material success of the times. Though the word guilt was seldom used, it was precisely this which was implicit in the relations between the two classes at this juncture. It is hard to believe that so ardent a generation of church-goers could have failed to apply moral principles to their own relationships with the poor, and it is significant that when the state of some wretched individual was unavoidably forced upon them, they reacted with a most uncharacteristic gesture of indiscriminate generosity.

Whatever its causes, the fashion for philanthropy swept over old families and new alike, goading men on, as Shimmin put it in one of his recurrent protests, " to give expression to ostentatious sentimentality, and lead[ing] them to neglect their legitimate duties. This is becoming a social nuisance, and men under its guidance are induced and encouraged to roam abroad in search of what is merely imaginary, to go dancing over all sorts of ground after the mere phantom of philanthropy."[28] The practical result was an

[27] *Porcupine*, 1st June, 1861.

[28] *Porcupine*, 1st December, 1860.

outbreak of what was nothing less than ill-informed and ill-inspired meddling with the working classes. Contemporary thinking was against any attempt to control individual freedom and though efforts to prevent overlapping or to fill in gaps were made, charity was commonly regarded as a matter for individual enterprise. Whoever saw a need was free to meet it according to his fancy, with results of which William Rathbone took a poor view; "hitherto, individualism has run riot in all voluntary effort, and in the privilege of mismanaging its own affairs claimed by every class and community among us."[29]

Large societies and small, with or without managing committees, raising funds as and how their sponsors thought fit, reporting on their labours at annual meetings of great respectability held in the Town Hall,[30] or conducted in a complete obscurity which frequently covered mismanagement if not false pretences, the sum total certainty merited its description as a maelstrom.[31]

Benevolence under such circumstances was not necessarily bogus or insincere but tended to be simply a relief to feelings of compassion. It was based on imitation of the methods rather than understanding of the aims of the "old families". This was particularly apparent in the increase of occasions for wholesale patronage such as Christmas parties and summer treats in the gardens of the new suburban residences of Aigburth, from which, however kindly their intention, the only excusable basis of mutual regard was frequently lacking. A typical example describes "treats for boy chimney sweeps, and for others who were 'down and out'. The chimney sweeps before their repast had a good bath in the stable copper where hot mashes were commonly boiled for the cows and horses. The younger James Cropper relates how when he himself was a boy he watched the whole process, and how the cowman scoured the sooty lads till their white skin became visible. After the bath fresh garments were given to them, fresh to them, but not for the most part new. Then they had a jorum of hot drink with a bottle of sherry poured into it, this being before the days of strict teetotalism, and then came a meal for the poor little climbers, to whom Dingle Bank might well have seemed as it did to many others

> "A midway station given
> For happy spirits to alight,
> Betwixt this earth and Heaven".[32]

[29] W. Rathbone, *op. cit.*, p. 128.

[30] Invariably held in January without regard to each other's arrangements, as *Porcupine* regularly deplored, e.g., 14th January, 1865.

[31] Samuel Smith, M.P., *My Life Work* (Hodder & Stoughton, 1902), p. 89.

[32] Connybeare, *op. cit.*, p. 47.

A series of articles in *Porcupine* in 1867 entitled *Byeways of Benevolence* gives a fair sample of the plethora of good works which now broke upon the poor. The Shoeblack Society, for example, aimed to help " the hordes of neglected and starving boys that jostle us in the streets, crouch at the doors of restaurants, slouch about the Exchange, turn somersaults by the side of omnibuses, or infest the dock quays."[33] Shoeblack brigades were formed, the members of which wore little red coats. The year's expenditure was £420, and the Committee consisted of a handful of respected business men. Another unostentatious effort was the Clog Club, of the " bubbling of whose little well of benevolence " *Porcupine* reported : " It is well known that there are many more deaths amongst the children of the poor than any other class; and this is brought about by insistent wet feet, as much as anything; it is also painful to see many limping along from wounds caused by treading on broken glass, nails, etc.; and frost is a great enemy to naked feet. A few gentlemen have joined together for the purpose of providing (as far as means will allow) common wooden clogs to some of the poor children; although aware that charity is open to abuse, they trust that their efforts to do a little good will not be entirely thrown away."[34]

There would seem, indeed, to have been provision for every imaginable need, including the prevention of cruelty to animals, and the installation of drinking fountains for human beings, his enthusiasm for which earned for one of the Melly family the nickname of Fountain Melly.

Whatever form it took, the bulk of all this work appears to have been done voluntarily. To work for payment of any kind was not an acceptable idea in a society whose basis for gentility was the possession of private means : to receive payment for doing one's duty would have been doubly degrading. Moreover, the Poor Law policy of rendering relief unattractive had led to the association of harshness with the idea of paid agents, and such employees as were retained were limited to the collection of subscriptions or the distribution of alms on the instruction of their employers, who regarded them as being in the category of superior house servants. Paid workers were more commonly employed in the religious field, as missioners, or scripture readers, but these were as a rule awarded small recompense for their labours.[35]

[33] *Porcupine*, 13th April, 1867.

[34] *Ibid.*, 12th January, 1867.

[35] As witness the advertisement for " a prudent painstaking, pious, devoted, and well-educated Female, without encumbrance, to labour among the poor in a south-end district. Will be required to reside near the church. The remuneration, 10s. per week, with a furnished room, coals, and gas." Quoted in *Porcupine*, 4th November, 1865.

E

The one thing which is noticeably absent from all this activity is any contribution by the poor themselves; the aim of the whole business was obviously to do things for them, a strange paradox in an age which worshipped individualism and self-help. The National Association for the Promotion of Social Science spoke approvingly of the papers contributed by Liverpool working men to the meeting in 1858, and agreed that "the great charm to the British operative is the privilege of self-government. For this he will risk his all ".[36] But of the practical application of this sentiment there is little sign. That this should have been so was in part due to the urgency of the problems of material relief, in part to the rapid degeneration of working class morale. There was in addition the intangible but real obstacle of the lack of mutual understanding between the classes. Ignorance of each other's daily lives, the gulf between those with leisure for culture and those with neither leisure nor culture, an excessive formalism of manner on the one hand contrasted with a distressing lack of any acquired wisdom or tradition on the other, these were barriers to any warmth of sympathy between patron and patronised.

"We know too little of the inward consciousness of the toiling and the suffering poor, to be able to speak with any confidence of their own view of their own existence ".[37]

The relationship with the poor was in consequence difficult and strained, and apart from the satisfaction derived by the poor man from individual contact with a member of the powerful propertied classes, the working classes had a good deal to put up with in the name of charity. The Domestic Missioners reported feelingly that "courteous visiting will ensure a courteous reception", and deplored the impatience of visitors who wished to force reformation upon the poor, forgetful of the fact "that they are in the house of another in the capacity of visitors ".[38] Of too many it could be said that "the intention of philanthropists is one thing, the manner in which they carry their intentions out—the way in which they meet and mingle with those whom they wish to benefit—is quite another. (The workingmen's) bluntness is often mistaken for impertinence, their earnestness looked upon as vulgarity and their demeanour spoken of as not being at all ' gentlemanly '."[39]

Meanwhile, underneath the froth and fashion, the steady flow of charitable effort continued much as it had always done, and *Porcupine* warned dabblers that their aspirations to membership of the exclusive "social" clique would very possibly involve them in having "to deal with some ruthless persons whose hearts are really

[36] Charles Hardwick, *Benefit Societies. Proceedings,* p. 639.
[37] Thom, *op. cit.,* p. 177.
[38] Domestic Mission Annual Report for 1855.
[39] *Porcupine,* 11th December, 1860.

in their work, and who will insist upon your undertaking some actual and uncomfortable duty which, if you cannot buy yourself off by a large subscription, you will infallibly have to attempt ".[40]

The diversion of charitable effort to the physical civilisation of the poor certainly succeeded in so far as it roused the public to a new interest in slum conditions. But no clear conception had emerged of what was to be done with this interest, or of how charity could be expressed in terms of material improvement.

This account is not concerned with assessing the extent to which the idea of physical regeneration diverted charitable effort into the struggle for social reform, nor is it possible to pursue here the increase in private benefactions for such public amenities as museums, parks and libraries which characterised the middle years of the century. Within the narrowly charitable sphere, although tribute was paid to " the importance of those sanitary arrangements which we know full well will tend to the diminution of pauperism ",[41] it proved difficult to interpret such principles in terms of charity rather than reform. True, under its influence, possibly more clogs than bibles were provided, but few concrete schemes to remedy any of the main material problems were put forward apart from one small effort to introduce lighting into dark courts.[42] Octavia Hill's work was much discussed, and housing was constantly cited as the underlying cause of social misery, but this gave rise to only one Labourers' Housing Scheme, the complicating factor of the docker's need to live near the docks proving decisive.[43]

To sum up the situation it may therefore be said that whereas in the field of public administration immense strides were made, in charitable work the characteristic note was one of bafflement. How could the appearance of the middle classes on the philanthropic scene be turned to a useful end? How could the belief that the proper object of charity was the material reform of the condition of the people be put into practice? What hope was there of science providing a solution to the problem of poverty? And if so, what of charity? To all these questions there seemed no obvious reply, and the way ahead was clouded by doubt and uncertainty. New factors were already at work, however, which were eventually to bring about the resolution of the situation. Of these, the contribution made by women was to prove outstanding, and to the movement for their emancipation in its relation to charitable work the next chapter is therefore devoted.

[40] *Ibid.,* 1st June, 1861.
[41] The Earl of Shaftesbury to the National Association for the Promotion of Social Science, Liverpool, 1858. *Proceedings,* p. 91.
[42] Postance, *op. cit.*
[43] Trench and Beard, *op. cit.*

CHAPTER V

WOMEN IN CHARITABLE WORK: "FEMININE PHILANTHROPY",
1850-1870

THE ideals of middle class society in the 1850's pressed heavily upon women. The daily round of the competent housewife, whose contribution to her husband's affairs had been to supervise the welfare of his dependents and employees, was no longer regarded as either desirable or even feasible. In place of these lost satisfactions, life in a community devoted to "getting on" had little to offer. Its inevitable formality and superficiality deprived it of emotional substance, its growing prudery of emotional satisfaction. The increasing prestige of idleness as the traditional characteristic of gentility, combined with the contemporary and contrary prestige attaching to industry, drove women into the extremes of time-filling ingenuity for which they have been derided ever since, and which the lack of facilities for female education did nothing to correct. Many of the new middle classes were women who, thirty years before, would never have presumed to keep a servant,[1] and who were ill-equipped to enjoy the leisure now thrust upon them for the first time.

However, it was when they ventured to look beyond the confines of their own homes that Victorian women became most acutely aware of the contraction of the world about them. Hampered by the current conception of how a lady should behave, and by their own inadequacy in situations outside their normal experience, they faced a progressive limitation of their opportunities for work in the world at large. Even if the dangers of infection and insult, and the obstacle of spatial distance between rich and poor could have been overcome, as they were by certain stalwarts amongst the Unitarians, for instance, there remained the inescapable fact that the poor were no longer so readily accessible to the exercise of charity. The tendency throughout the century had been towards handling the poor in the mass as the only means of dealing with their enormous numbers but this had had the effect of removing to institutions those upon whom women had been accustomed to exercise their "natural" functions of loving and cherishing. In such institutions, lady visitors were not welcomed. Thus the Liverpool Vestry had, in 1854[2] forbidden ladies to visit the Brownlow Hill Workhouse as a result of the report made by a chaplain that ladies of another

[1] Hugh Shimmin, *Domestic Servants*. A Paper read before the Liverpool Association for the Promotion of Social Science. 1862.

[2] *Liverpool Courier*, 1st February, 1854.

denomination had been found reading a bible beside the sick bed of an inmate.

Though some of these institutions had long had committees of supporting ladies, and the Ladies Charity,[3] was actually administered by women, the scope offered was limited, and the responsible male never far to seek, firmly enforcing the distinction between men's responsibilities and those suitable for women. The Liverpool Benevolent Institution for Reclaiming Women and Girls, even after it came under the competent patronage of a Mrs. William Rathbone, included in its Fundamental Rules the proviso that the Gentlemen's Committee should audit the accounts, write the Annual Report, and approve the Minutes, to which was unofficially added the duty of correcting the Secretary's spelling where necessary.[4]

Women were thus forced out of the field of practical social work, and were limited in the main to what they could undertake in their own homes, such as sewing garments for the poor or, amongst the higher-principled, cutting out garments the gift of which would, it was hoped, tempt the poor into doing some sewing on their own behalf. Working for bazaars and money-raising efforts provided a heaven-sent excuse for all manner of activities which would otherwise have been forbidden to the correctly behaved young lady. Charity sermons and the solicitation of subscriptions from relatives yielded place to the Fancy Fair, the Bazaar, and the wide variety of concert party, musical evening and charity ball, a process which *Porcupine* eyed with disfavour, quoting instances from which no profit at all accrued to the charity concerned[5] but which rendered inestimable service by providing a use for otherwise aimless accomplishments.

Though many would have denied it, and did in fact do so, Josephine Butler's analysis of the society in which she found herself in Liverpool was shrewd. "The great tide of an imperfect and halting civilisation has rolled onward, and carried many triumphantly with it. But women have been left stranded, so to speak . . . The wave has passed them by. Their work is taken out of their hands: their place—they know not where it is. They stretch out their hands idly."[6] It must have been a baffling experience for women to find themselves frustrated in such times of opportunity, unsatisfied in such an age of plenty, discontented amidst such universal complacency.

Women were not, of course, totally excluded from the practice

[3] See p. 21.
[4] 69th Annual Report, 1908.
[5] e.g., 12th March, 1870.
[6] *Woman's Work and Woman's Culture.* Edited by Josephine Butler (Macmillan & Co., 1869), pp. xv and xxiii.

of charity, and there were outstanding women whose social position
and religious principles gave them the assurance necessary to
behaving as their conscience dictated, regardless of public opinion.[7]
Sarah Willink, the second daughter of Edward Cropper "had a class
of sixty working men, for whom she built an outside room, to which
for many years these men trooped in, Sunday after Sunday, from
the neighbouring streets (not without protest from some of the
inhabitants of Dingle Bank)"[8] The District Provident Society relied
on such women for its collectors and the Domestic Mission for its
Sunday School teachers, and the obituary notices of women like
Mrs. Rathbone and Mrs. Melly make it plain that their lives were
far from being cabined and confined.[9]

Nevertheless, it was in these very circles where the tradition
of social responsibility, combined with a high regard for the things
of the mind, might have been expected to ensure adequate opportunities for women, that awareness of the limitations imposed
by their sex was most acutely felt. Obviously the women's movement owed the new life which now infused it to some desperation
bred specifically by middle class life. It bore little relation for many
years to come to the demands of working class women for a living
wage, but though it lacked the urgency of the cry of the poor it was
none the less desperate. "The demand of the women of the humbler
classes for bread may be more pressing, but it is no more sincere,
than that of the women of the better classes for work".[10]

It is thus no mere co-incidence that one of the pioneers of the
movement for emancipation should have been the daughter of a
Liverpool cotton merchant, though it is fortunate that the record of
her life and thoughts should be available in a diary kept by Miss
Anne Jemima Clough,[11] who later became the first Principal of
Newnham College. This is doubly valuable in that it expresses both
the reaction of contemporary women to their own position and of
the benevolent to the poverty of others, making strikingly plain the
connection between the two.

Born in Rodney Street in 1820, her father's interests as a cotton
merchant led to Miss Clough's childhood being spent in South

---

[7] Of whom Mrs. Carlyle wrote: "Most of the company were Unitarians;
the men with faces like a meat-axe; the women most palpably without
bustles—a more unlovable set of human beings I never looked on".
J. Estlin Carpenter, quoted in *James Martineau* (Philip Green, 1905), p.
260.

[8] Connybeare, *op. cit.* p. 43.

[9] It was said of the sixth William Rathbone, for instance, that he " never
reached an important decision and rarely made a speech or wrote a letter
of consequence without consulting [his wife]." *Liverpool Daily Post*,
20th March, 1918.

[10] *Woman's Work*, p. xxiii.

[11] Quoted in the *Memoir of Anne J. Clough*. By her niece, Blanche Athena
Clough (Edward Arnold, 1897).

Carolina where her early religious development was intensified by the controversy over slavery. It was inevitable that on her return to Liverpool in 1836 she should be acutely aware of social obligations towards that other class of depressed persons, the poor. Seeking for some practical means of expressing this obligation, and being of Welsh origin, she undertook to teach in the Welsh National School, gradually extending her activities to visiting the parents, inviting girls to her own home, and taking children from the workhouse for walks. Meanwhile her status as a merchant's daughter offered her pleasant prospects, while the influence of her brother Arthur Hugh Clough, inspired her to undertake a programme of severe intellectual discipline. Her conscience, her emotions, her intellect, thus stimulated, she was subjected to an inner conflict for which there seemed no obvious solution.

" I would often fain stay at home and read my books. However, duty must then come in and take the command; my weak heart often recoils from going into many of the scenes of misery about; it grows lazy in its work, and would fain rest. I do see misery sometimes till I am quite heart-sick. The thoughts of marriage and such things do certainly come very often into my mind now. I have still a great hankering after learning Greek ".[12]

Her charitable work was inspired by a sense of duty in the first place, but the satisfaction she derived from it was not merely ease of conscience, and she was evidently able to answer her own question as to motive: " I don't see that we are to have any motive in this, but that the love which is in us makes us do all this naturally, and constrains us to work. Is not this the Spirit of God which stirs in our hearts? "[13] It gave her the horrors to go visiting the slums, yet she derived on occasion immense pleasure from the warmth of her relations with those whom she came to call her friends, a warmth the lack of which in the social life of her own class led her to utter the cry, echoed by so many young women, " I feel myself much better fitted for holding intercourse with the poor. I don't get on in a drawing-room ".[14] In charitable work, too, she found some relief from the hunger of the idle woman to be valued as an individual; she was quite disproportionately moved by the fact that " the children know me, and speak my name. This was delicious to me, and worth more than a thousand praises. This was one of my grandest days; it was almost too much for me ".[15]

Refusal to face the futility of their existence was characteristic of many women; in Miss Clough it took the form of ambitious longings to do something to ensure that her name would be remembered

[12] *Ibid.*, p. 34.
[13] *Ibid*, p. 39
[14] *Ibid.*, p. 76.
[15] *Ibid.*, p. 22.

by future generations, but of this ambition, she felt frustrated by being a wonan in a man's world. She was miserably conscious of the limitations imposed by her sex, and this, together with the fact that she lived largely with women, her father being dead and her brother often from home, created a gulf between her and the men she met which might well have turned into open antagonism, a possibility the subsequent story of the women's movement was to demonstrate.

Yet all the time, her head was filled with thoughts of marriage, jostling the Greek and German aside while she studied, tempting her to take her pleasures as she could and leave the poor to their own devices. Walking up the fashionable Bold Street, she felt that she was the focus of admiration; when she went to parties her eager anticipation made it all the more bitter that she could not talk well to gentlemen. The convention of her times bade her reprimand herself for indulgence in dreams of " love and such things ": this, and her ill-success in society, drove her back to her studies, determined, by being " more and more secret and retired ", to defend herself from the unseemly play of her emotions. This fortified her natural inclination towards intellectual pursuits, which in a woman, was regarded as sufficiently odd to call for comment. " I certainly don't know why I do try to learn so many things, and spend time thus, but I feel a great impulse to do so, therefore I think I must ".[16]

Racked in turn by the strong forces within her, which made it impossible for her to accept the restrictions of her life, and drove her to seek their expression in first one direction and then another, Miss Clough was very conscious of loneliness in her struggles with herself, and of the lack of any guidance from those about her. Finally, the demands of her intelligence, the fact that family misfortunes had led her to open a small school and the inevitable ill-success of so original a character in local society, led her on to the last stage in her long progress towards emancipation, when she openly discussed with her brother whether it could be " right in certain cases to quit even one's father and mother and family for work as well as for a husband".[17]

Years passed before she felt that the moment had come to put this theory into practice, and by that time she had moved away from Liverpool. This move seems to have marked a significant stage in career for on leaving Liverpool she abandoned her diary, and was evidently, to use her own words. " waiting silent, watchful and alert for the moment when the great change could be made with the least hurt to the feelings and prejudices of those nearest and dearest to them."[18]

[16] *Ibid.,* p. 28.
[17] *Ibid.,* p. 63.
[18] *Ibid.,* p. 254.

There is no reason to suppose that Miss Clough's state of mind was in any way uncommon. Looking back on her early life, she talked in general terms of herself and her contemporaries, taking for granted the common nature of her own experiences, whilst the keen intellectual life of the leading merchant families forbids the suggestion that Liverpool alone amongst provincial cities was exempt from awareness of the gathering restlessness among women. As has already been pointed out, it was in precisely such circles that women were most keenly aware of their disabilities.

Many, of course, simply accepted their lot, lacking that knowledge or experience of any other way of life which might have stimulated them to protest. Unaware of any sense of social obligation, they concentrated on keeping up appearances, thus earning the scathing criticism of *Porcupine*, who deplored the expense involved in their support by the young man who married into his own class, and the consequent tendency to seek female companionship elsewhere. The Public Library, meanwhile, found itself faced with such an increase in the number of novel-reading females as to create quite a problem though it did not despair of their progress to more serious literature. But there were also those who, like Miss Clough, were " stirred by the awakening of thought around them, by the new interest in social reform . . . they grew restless, they were like caged birds, with their strong passions intensified by the want of action . . . living together in dull contracted surroundings, in homes where there was not enough occupation for all, [they] were restless and unhappy, and struggled for they knew not what. Some had none to give them sympathy and help, and had not courage or wit to find out and enter on new paths for themselves. . . . Many suffered grievously, some fell into ill-health, many were soured and spent their lives in foolish and useless complaining ".[19]

To such women, the last straw was their own impotence in the face of the unparalleled distress of the late 'forties, and the charitable work of women at this period is marked by the coming together of small groups who sought to gain strength from each other in order to overcome their individual disabilities. An illustration of this is provided by the admirable records which the Jewish Ladies' Benevolent Institution, alone amongst so many, have carefully preserved for over a century. The Institution was founded in 1849 to enable women of the Jewish community to take a practical interest in their poorer sisters during sickness and confinement. They so far distrusted their own capacity that they relied upon the services of a male Honorary Secretary for many years, till, goaded by his lack of zeal, they ousted him in favour of Mrs. David Lewis (wife of the founder of the stores which bear his name), a process which evidently filled

[19] *Ibid.*, p. 96.

him with indignant surprise, to judge by Mrs. Lewis's mock-demure account of her efforts to present to him the testimonial demanded by propriety if not by gratitude. Even after this declaration of emancipation, however, the Jewish Ladies clung to the support of a gentleman's committee in raising their funds, and to the main benevolent association of their religious body for guidance in spending them.

So far as the work consisted of the housewifely tasks of organising the services of doctors and nurses, arranging for the loan of bedding, and for the making up and distributing of clothing, the Jewish Ladies were more than equal to their task, but the recurrent discussion of the purposes for which their funds should be used indicate a growing bewilderment as to the proper objects of their charity. It was easy to rule that only cases of sickness of a temporary character should be considered, and that those cases must be Jewish women resident in Liverpol, who were both deserving and of good character, and, in cases of confinement, were able to produce satisfactory evidence of marriage. However, in practice, the investigation of cases by untrained volunteers proved so difficult and so unsavoury, and the conflict of pity and principle involved in each decision so baffling and painful, that only the most valiant of the members continued their active service, the rest tending to absent themselves upon such reasonable excuse as their disinclination to remain in town during the insanitary summer months. The Minutes of the meetings are a tribute to those who plodded on, bravely endeavouring to reconcile themselves to the discovery that the poor were so frequently not also the deserving, and to combine correct charitable practice with natural commonsense, as in the case of the poor woman, Mary Cohen, who in her commendable endeavour to earn a living, incurred a fine of 7s. 6d. for selling spoliges[20] without a licence.

Further evidence of an attempt to adapt their services to the contemporary situation is provided by the campaign to secure the re-admission of women as visitors to the Workhouse. This was an obvious step, in view of the interest which had been taken in Poor Law reform throughout the century, and the fact that in an institution the poor were presented in a coherent group, so that the problems of contacting them were automatically overcome.

Reports to the meeting of the National Association for the Promotion of Social Science held in Liverpool in 1858, of the schemes for the voluntary visiting of inmates of Poor Law institutions in St. Pancras and elsewhere, led to a request that the Vestry should institute a formal scheme for lady visitors to the Brownlow Hill Workhouse. The lead was taken by Mr. George Melly, who proposed at a meeting of the Vestry[21] that the ban of 1854 be

[20] Presumably spoiled goods (Shorter Oxford English Dictionary).
[21] *Liverpool Mercury*, 10th November, 1858.

rescinded and that those ladies be admitted "in whom the committee had entire confidence that they would act with discretion", their services to be limited to acts of kindliness, consolation and advice. Mr. Melly's resolution was duly referred to the Workhouse Committee to whom he reported that a scheme had been prepared.[22] The scheme invited ladies resident in Liverpool and its neighbourhood, who wished to devote one or two mornings a week to visiting the inmates, to send in their names to the Committee, who would choose from amongst them twelve to serve for one year as "lady Visitors to the Liverpool Workhouse". Should they absent themselves for three consecutive months, their places were to be filled, a penalty which applied equally to those whose visits proved unwelcome to the Committee for any reason. Each lady was to be given an extract of the Poor Law Board's orders relating to discipline in the house, together with instructions specially prepared for their guidance which began with the warning that: —

"As many persons, judging from past experience, consider that the dangers of introducing an organized system of lady visitors may outweigh the advantages, however great they undoubtedly are, and as it has been proved on more than one occasion that one mistake will over-balance much benefit, the greatest prudence and care will be necessary on the part of the lady visitors".

These it was hoped would not unduly hamper the lady visitors, and might "lessen the dangers of collision and discomfort on the part of the officials, visitors or inmates". It is an anti-climax to find that the rules to which this was a prelude merely require that remarks on management should be made only to the Committee, that each lady should mark out a beat in certain wards and stick to it as far as possible, and that the spirit of dissension should not be roused. The fuss was not of course wholly due to timidity regarding the admission of ladies as such but owed a good real to the constant religious dissension which pervaded the administration of the Poor Law.

What the ladies made of it all is, as usual, not recorded, though one of them, in applying to the Committee for permission to serve as a visitor, wrote an interesting letter explaining her motives and objects in so doing, and obviously drafted to placate the opposition on the committee. It opens with a firm declaration that she does not visualise herself in the role of a clergyman, but as a fellow-mortal bringing the humanising influence of sympathy to bear upon the aged and sick. For her experience in ordinary district visiting had taught her that as a rule "the poor are ever thankful for, and sensible to, the influence of those to whom education and other causes have given a superior degree of refinement. Mere interest and sympathy,

[22] *Liverpool Mercury,* 12th November, 1858.

such as are called forth by our ordinary every-day intercourse with those of our own class, tell greatly upon the poor when carried into their homes by those whom they recognise as their superiors, and yet know to be working voluntarily amongst them ".[23]

Unfortunately, the subsequent history of the scheme is not known.[24] The list of visitors indicates that it was carefully compiled to include only experienced women, already associated with local charitable institutions and suitably distributed amongst the various denominations. These ladies were called together to meet members of the committee, and received instructions from the Governor of the Workhouse, who reported two months later that apart from minor indiscretions due to inexperience, such as the distribution of tracts, the scheme was working well. Probably the care which had been exercised in the choice of visitors defeated its own object, for women of the calibre of those put forward by the Unitarians, for example, were hardly likely to find satisfaction in the limited scope offered to them. They must quickly have become aware of the deficiencies of the institution as a solution to the problems of poverty, and were consequently eager to support Mr. Rathbone's scheme for nursing the sick poor in their own homes.

Though the District Nursing Society was not a direct response to the need for opportunities for public service by women, and Mr. Rathbone was emphatic that " where women have families, there is their proper field, and we seek no help at the cost of neglected duties,"[25] yet its administration was nevertheless deliberately based on the existence of a class of leisured women and constituted a challenge to that organising of the poor into institutions to which reference has already been made.[26]

Deeply moved as he then was by the illness and death of his first wife, Mr. Rathbone determined in 1859 to discover how far the nursing which she had enjoyed could be extended to the poor in their own homes. True to his tradition, his experiment was simple and unostentatious; knowing from experience the quality of his wife's nurse, he simply asked her to undertake at his expense to nurse certain poor patients in their homes for a limited period. Mr. Rathbone's own description of his experiment has been so often quoted

[23] *Liverpool Daily Post*, 24th November, 1859.

[24] Though a Miss Thorburn, in evidence to the Royal Commission on the Poor Laws, stated that when women were first elected to the Board of Guardians in 1894, the practice of appointing ladies as visitors was allowed to lapse.   Appendix, Vol. iv. Cd. 4835, 1909, p. 8.

[25] *Organisation of Nursing*. By a member (William Rathbone) of the Committee of the Home and Training School (Longman, Green, 1865), p. 49.

[26] " One can comfort them in their cottages, and give them food and medicine, but to nurse and heal them there with any prospect of success cannot be done ". Contemporary opinion, quoted at the Jubilee Congress of District Nursing, Liverpool, 1909.

as to become a classic, but it bears repetition for no other words could convey more exactly the atmosphere of his philanthropy.

"As this was only an experiment, the nurse was not engaged for more than three months. But when one month was passed, she returned to her employer and entreated to be released from the engagement. Accustomed though she was to many forms of sickness and death, she was not able to endure the sight of the misery which she had encountered among the poor. But her employer persuaded her to persevere in her work, and pointed out to her how much of the evil which she had seen might be prevented, and that the satisfaction of abating it would in time be sure to reconcile her to the work. Thus reasoned with, the nurse persevered, and at the end of three months entirely corroborated the prediction. She found that she was able to do great and certain good, and the satisfaction of her achievements was so great that she begged to be allowed to devote herself entirely to nursing the poor in the place of nursing wealthy families ".[27]

Satisfied that the basic idea of a home nursing service was sound, Mr. Rathbone accepted the obligation " to continue and extend the work which had such a successful beginning. There was, fortunately, no doubt that the necessary funds would be forthcoming, but there was another drawback of a serious nature; the skilled nurses—without whom funds were useless—could nowhere be obtained ".[28] Learning from Florence Nightingale that his only hope of securing competent nurses lay in having them trained locally, and further discovering that the chairman of the governing body of the Royal Infirmary was reputed to be conservative in outlook, and therefore unlikely to take the necessary action, he patiently started by securing his own election as a governor. Visiting with the chairman on the first possible day, he realised that it was less lack of enterprise than lack of accommodation which held back the governing body from instituting a training school for nurses. This, he states quietly, his savings enabled him to remedy. The planning and building of the Home were given his usual time and thought. In 1863, only four years after the original experiment, the first annual report of the Liverpool Training School and Home for Nurses was published, covering the training of nurses for hospital, district and private nursing, and the working of the first twelve districts.

Having thus ensured the supply of nurses, Mr. Rathbone proceeded with his original scheme for nursing the poor in their own homes, which was based on the personal responsibility of each Lady Superintendent for the district entrusted to her care. By this means it was hoped to avoid the evils of nationalised or institutionalised

---

[27] William Rathbone, M.P., *The History and Progress of District Nursing* (Macmillan & Co., 1890), p. 14 *et seq.*
[28] *Ibid.*, p. 14.

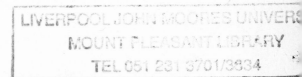

service, of which the most often quoted were extravagant administration and the lack of the human touch.[29] The Lady Superintendents' duties were most carefully defined. " In each district a lady, or a
committee of ladies was provided to superintend the work, but these
ladies were not required to have any professional knowledge of
nursing. They undertook to provide the medical comforts required,
to find lodgings for the nurse in a good central situation, and—in
beginning the work in a new district—a meeting of the clergy and
ministers of the various religious bodies, and others living in the
district, was called in order to explain to them the nature of the
objects aimed at, and to request that they would interest their friends
and parishioners in the work. The Lady Superintendent was herself
provided with a map of the district, a nurse's register book and
forms of recommendation and application. She was to visit, either
in person or by deputy, all cases under treatment, so as to obtain
assurance that the nurse was working faithfully and well. From time
to time she was to examine the nurse's register, to consult with her
on fresh cases, and to hear her report on old ones. It was her duty
to arrange for the supply, custody and distribution of medical comforts and appliances, and to keep memoranda of all expenses
incurred, and of articles lent ".[30]

The standard set for these voluntary workers was high, and
Charles Langton, who succeeded Mr. Rathbone as Honorary Secretary, was later able to say that in the thirty-five years in which the
finding of volunteers for the work had been his special care, " there
were hardly ever districts without Lady Superintendents, and that
of the ladies on the list in 1898 six had held this office for over thirty
years, namely Mrs. W. Rathbone, Mrs. C. Langton, Mrs. H. G.
Gilmour, Mrs. Paget, Mrs. George Holt, and the late Mrs. R. D.
Holt ".[31]

The reports of the Lady Superintendents were included in the
Annual Reports; they convey an impression of the competence of
women used to considerable domestic responsibility, and with the
assured social position which takes the sting out of money-raising,
and the need for publicity out of benevolence. They do not hesitate
to admit that the Ladies have much to learn, that of course they are
deceived by some clients, but that this will be remedied as they and
the nurses gain experience. Their honesty is refreshing: " I have
but few remarks to make respecting this district, indeed I wish I had

---

[29] William Rathbone was described by Florence Nightingale as being " a
master hand in securing unity yet independence of action, that personal
responsibility and yet liberty so essential to continuance and development of a great charity." *Organisation of Nursing.* Introduction, p. 9.

[30] *History and Progress of District Nursing*, p. 25.

[31] Delegates' Local Handbook. Jubilee Congress of District Nursing.
Liverpool, 1909.

more to say, for I fear we are getting into a routine which results mainly in dispensing chops, beef-tea, sago, rice, tea and sugar . . . I do not believe the right class of cases come into our hands in this district. I am completely at a loss to account for this . . . "[32]

The work was carried out under an almost complete anonymity, the names of the Committee and Lady Superintendents being given simply " in order to keep up the public interest and the confidence of subscribers ".[33] Neither departure from Liverpool, nor even death itself, merited more than the briefest reference in the Reports to the loss of a worker of however many years standing. Such an excess of modesty verges on the peculiar unless it is remembered that it was at this time that benevolence was becoming fashionable, and its motives consequently subject to open cynicism. Such names as do appear indicate that the service was supported largely by the Rathbone family and their immediate circle.

Funds for running the districts were the responsibility of local congregations, employers, and others with local affiliations, but in practice at least seven were entirely supported by the Lady Superintendents and their immediate families.[34] The sums raised varied from £60 to £120 a year; in some districts " those other agencies were at hand, provided, for the most part, out of the same purses and superintended to a great extent by the same ladies ".[35]

The system was in full operation by 1865 though some of the eighteen Districts had to depend on partially trained nurses. There was for a long time misunderstanding on the part of the clergy and possible subscribers as to the nature of the service, which was commonly supposed to be merely one more relief agency. As Florence Nightingale put it, they had " to drag the noble art of nursing out of the sink of relief doles ".[36] The nurses themselves, especially before the standards of their profession began to stabilize, tended to let pity overwhelm them, and the Reports contain frequent comments on the need to restrain nurses from ordering food for their patients, with as a corollary, a growing if somewhat astonished appreciation, which the Ladies themselves seem to have shared, of the value of milk. Relief was given where it was evident that nursing alone could not achieve recovery, but there was constant co-operation with the Central Relief Society and similar agencies in the endeavour to pass this duty on to others. The Ladies seem to have steered a sensible middle course on this as on other difficult questions, gradually educating themselves, the doctors, and the patients as to the

[32] Annual Report, 1864.
[33] *Organization of Nursing*, p. 64.
[34] *Organization of Nursing*, p. 57.
[35] Annual Report, 1865.
[36] *History and Progress of District Nursing*.

proper use of the nurses. " I think my nurse would agree," says one in the Report of 1877 ". . . that if there were no cooking to be done, nor food to give out, there would not have been full work in my district; but, if we did *not* cook, and give food, there would be far more sickness than there is."

The one thing Mr. Rathbone failed to foresee was that the existence side by side of professional and voluntary workers would result in competition which the ladies were ill-equipped to face. As paid employees, the District Nurses inherited something like the relationship of maid to mistress when they first began work. However, the distinction between a lady and a nurse was gradually obliterated, and the patronage by the lady of a paid employee changed to respect for the member of a skilled profession. What Mr. Rathbone called the "naturally feminine" aspects of the work became increasingly the province of the trained nurses, the ladies being left with the heavy and not at all womanly burdens of finance and administration, which to their credit, they long carried without complaint. It was in fact, their success in extending the service which was to become the cause of their own elimination. It would be interesting to pursue further this question of the relationship between professional and voluntary workers in charitable effort: had there been a Florence Nightingale to impress upon Mr. Rathbone the necessity for trained personnel for the relief schemes to which he next turned his attention, the subsequent history of social welfare would have run very differently.

Of the extent to which such forms of service gave a sense of fulfilment to the ladies concerned, no record exists, for discretion was a universal rule. In any case, the fact that organized forms of philanthropy tended to become the private preserve of the particular clique amongst the local aristocracy who had been responsible for their initiation meant that work under their auspices was open to comparatively few. The numbers outside this closed circle were meanwhile steadily growing, and of their state of mind direct evidence is available in the autobiography of one of the outstanding figures of the movement for the emancipation of women. Josephine Butler never secured for herself a place in local society,[37] and her intensity of emotion was, of course, entirely individual, but this does not render any less valuable the picture she presents of the life of middle class women in the Liverpool of her times. Nor can her appearance on the scene be set aside as simply one of those fortunate coincidences which befall the lucky historian, for she was essentially the product of her time and place.

From her own account of her early life, Josephine Butler must long have been fascinated and shocked by the implications of the

[37] There still lingers a tradition that one had to know Mrs. Butler because of her husband's connection with the College.

differing status of the men and women of her generation. " Not but what the happiest among us have not observed and pondered with amazement, from our very childhood, on certain customs, laws, and maxims prevalent among us, which seem only to recognize the existence of one half of the human family ".[38] Wherein this sense of injustice originated, it is impossible now to perceive, but it is interesting that, like Miss Clough, Josephine Butler was brought into daily contact with the movement for the emancipation of slaves at an early age, her father being a keen abolitionist. The conflict between what she believed with passionate conviction to be the natural heritage of every human being, and what in reality was permitted to women, was to dominate her whole life, and made it inevitable that her efforts to find in philanthropy a solution of her personal problem should be directed into the campaign against that most bitter inequality of the sexes with which her name has since become identified.

Her salvation lay, possibly, in her good fortune in finding for a husband a man of whom she could write, " Had that work been purely a product of the feminine mind, of a solitary, wounded and revolted heart, it would certainly have lacked some elements essential to its becoming in any way useful or fruitful. But for him I should have been much more perplexed than I was. The idea of justice to women, of equality between the sexes and of equality of responsibility of all human beings to the moral law, seems to have been instinctive in him. He never needed convincing ".[39] In spite of this, she never reconciled herself to the implications of her status as a married woman. The outward acceptance of the tacit assumption of superiority by her husband's Oxford colleagues demanded of her such an intensity of self control as could only find recompense in the bringing right into her own home of outstanding cases of unhappiness suffered by women at the hands of men. Yet constant ill health at this time suggests that even so, she was able to enjoy little peace of mind. The conflict between reason and reality assumed intolerable proportions when to the sense of injury done to her sex by the passing in 1864 of the Contagious Diseases Act permitting the State regulation of vice in this country, was added the personal catastrophe of the death of her only daughter who, running from an upstairs room to greet her mother, fell over the bannisters and died that same night. It must have been difficult for the distracted mind of a bereaved mother not to see in the loss of the only girl in a family of boys a symbol of the injustice done to all women.

Shortly after this, in 1866, the Rev. George Butler was invited to become Principal of Liverpool College, then the leading local school

[38] *Woman's Work*, p. xxvi.

[39] G. W. and Lucy Johnson, *Josephine Butler* (J. W. Arrowsmith Ltd., 1951), p. 34.

F

for boys, an invitation which he hastened to accept, no doubt in part because of the chance it offered of leaving the scene of such great unhappiness. However, mere change of surroundings was no remedy for Mrs. Butler's state of mind. The fact that her husband and the boys went off daily about their own affairs, leaving her alone and aimless to find such means as she could of occupying her time and her thoughts, simply added fuel to the fires of her burning sense of deprivation. Music, art, reading, all failed to alleviate the burden of her days. The constricted society of the new Sefton Park suburb where they lived coincided all too closely with her own feelings of frustration, and drove her to desperate efforts to escape on half-holidays by taking her family by train to North Wales and Derbyshire. At last, like so many more, she sought to ease the anguish of her personal unhappiness by contact with the unhappiness of others, no doubt influenced in this by her cousin, Charles Birrell, a brilliant ascetic, father of the essayist and an outstanding figure in local non-conformist circles. " I became possessed with an irresistible desire to go forth and find some pain keener than my own, to meet with people more unhappy than myself . . . I had no clear idea beyond that, no plan for helping others; my sole wish was to plunge into the heart of some human misery, and to say (as I now knew I could) to afflicted people, ' I understand : I too have suffered '. "[40]

Charles Birrell was at this time concerned with the provision of religious services for dissenting inmates of Poor Law Institutions, and he was presumably responsible for Mrs. Butler's introduction to the Brownlow Hill Workhouse, though there is no evidence that she was officially enrolled as an approved visitor. But it was surely by her own choice that she made straight for those most difficult and unruly work-sheds which were all that the baffled authorities could devise for dealing with the numbers of destitute women and girls then hanging about the streets of Liverpool :[41]

" It was not difficult to find misery in Liverpool. There was an immense workhouse containing at that time, it was said, five thousand persons—a little town in itself. The general hospital for paupers included in it was blessed in it by the angelic presence of Agnes Jones . . . ;[42] but the other departments in the great building were not so well organised as they came to be some years later. There were extensive special wards, where unhappy girls drifted like autumn leaves when the winter approached, many of them to die of

[40] *Ibid.*, p. 58.
[41] *Liverpool Daily Courier*, 13th September, 1865.
[42] Agnes Jones, a Nightingale nurse whom William Rathbone persuaded to undertake, at his expense, the difficult task of Lady Superintendent at the Brownlow Hill Workhouse in 1865, in order to convince the Vestry of the necessity for trained nurses. She died of typhus in 1868. See Eleanor Rathbone, *op. cit.*, pp. 168-173.

consumption, little cared for spiritually, for over this portion of the hospital Agnes Jones was not the presiding genius. There was on the ground floor a Bridewell for women, consisting of huge cellars, bare and unfurnished, with damp stone floors. These were called "the oakum sheds", and to these came voluntarily creatures driven by hunger, destitution, or vice, begging for a few nights' shelter and a piece of bread in return for which they picked their allotted portion of oakum. Others were sent there as prisoners.

"I went down to the oakum sheds and begged admission. I was taken into an immense gloomy vault filled with women and girls—more than two hundred probably at that time. I sat on the floor among them and picked oakum. They laughed at me, and told me my fingers were of no use for that work, which was true. But while we laughed we became friends. I proposed that they should learn a few verses to say to me on my next visit. I recollect a tall, dark, handsome girl standing up in our midst, among the damp refuse and lumps of tarred rope, and repeating without a mistake and in a not unmusical voice, clear and ringing, that wonderful fourteenth chapter of St. John's Gospel—the words of Jesus—all through, ending with, "Peace I leave with you. My peace I give unto you. Let not your heart be troubled, neither let it be afraid . . ." She had selected it herself, and they listened in perfect silence, this audience —wretched, draggled, ignorant, criminal, some wild, and defiant others. The tall, dark-haired girl had prepared the way for me, and I said, "now let us all kneel and cry to the same Jesus who spoke those words"; and down on their knees they fell, every one of them, reverently, on that damp stone floor, some saying the words after me, others moaning and weeping. It was a strange sound, that united wail—continuous, pitiful, strong—like a great sigh or murmur of vague desire and hope, issuing from the heart of despair, piercing the gloom and murky atmosphere of that vaulted room, and reaching to the heart of God ".[43]

She goes on to say that this drew down upon her such an avalanche of miserable but grateful womanhood that she had to stop to take breath and consider what practical help could be provided. Her widowed sister was staying with her at the time.

"We had a dry cellar in our house, and a garret or two, and into these we crowded as many as possible of the most friendless girls who were anxious to make a fresh start. This became inconvenient, and so in time my husband and I ventured to take a house near our own, trusting to find funds to furnish and fill it with inmates. This was "the House of Rest" . . . originally intended for the "poor, limp, fibreless human weeds" but gradually used for the incurable ".[44]

[43] Johnson, *op. cit.*, p. 57.
[44] *Ibid.*, p. 57.

Mrs. Butler was, however, not of the temperament to rest content in the service of the incurable. Convinced by her own experience that philanthropy was too largely devoted to draining off the worst of the pool of human misery rather than to stopping its inflow, she threw herself into a scheme for providing such training and employment as would prevent active young women from ever becoming charges upon charity.

" A few months later, encouraged by the help offered by a certain number of generous Liverpool merchants and other friends, we took a very large and solid house, with some ground round it, to serve as an industrial home for the healthy and active, the barefooted sand girls, and other friendless waifs and strays. We had a good gathering of friends and neighbours at a service which my husband held at the opening of the industrial home. His " dedication prayer " on that occasion was very touching, and full of kindness and heart-yearning towards the poor disinherited beings whom we desired to gather in. This house was very soon filled, and was successfully managed by an excellent matron, a mother. Besides the usual laundry and other work, we were able to set up a little envelope factory in one of the spacious rooms. This work called out some skill and nicety, and interested the girls very much. Several tradesmen and firms bought our envelopes at wholesale prices, and we also supplied some private friends disposed to help us . . . "[45]

Had she simply been grieving for a lost daughter, the work involved in caring for these other " lost " girls might well have brought her relief and eventually happiness. As it was, increased knowledge of the lives lived by her fellow women merely brought home to her more vividly the implications of the personal problem from which she had sought to escape. Active though she was in voluntary service, she felt that no opportunity existed for her to contribute as a woman to the solution of the major social problems. The futility of the Lady Bountiful she was willing to concede, but she feared that the " wholesale manipulation " of the poor which was succeeding it might prove equally harmful, all the more so because of its exclusion of service by women.

" We have had experience of what we may call the feminine form of philanthropy, and independent individual ministering, of too mediaeval a type to suit the present day. It has failed. We are now about to try the masculine form of philanthropy—large and comprehensive measures, organizations and systems planned by men and sanctioned by Parliament. This also will fail if it so far prevail as to extinguish the truth to which the other method witnessed in spite of its excesses. Why should we not try at last a union of principles which are equally true?".[46]

[45] *Ibid.*, p. 62
[46] *Woman's Work*, p. xxxvii.

Meanwhile, her connection with the College was giving her an insight into the lives of women in the new middle classes of Liverpool, which convinced her that there also lay " broken hearts, the deep discouragement and dismay, the deadness of souls, the destruction of moral natures ".[47] The lack of education for daughters of such families filled her with indignation and she was not altogether surprised though deeply shocked to find amongst them a number of cases of actual prostitution.

" It is not in their case a positive lack of a meal for today that drives them to this, but it is their generally exposed condition, the presence of temptation to frivolity, the absence of all mental resource, empty-headedness, love of dress, and the craving for some little affair of the heart to enliven the insipidity of their lives ".[48]

In an effort to remedy the lack of mental stimulus in women's lives, she accepted the Presidency of the North of England Council for the Higher Education of Women[49] as secretary of which Miss Clough was then serving her apprenticeship in educational reform. But though Mrs. Butler was convinced of the importance of education for women, the organization of lectures on astronomy and similar activities failed to satisfy the urgency of her inner compulsion to strike a blow at the very roots of inequality. The introduction which, as editor, she contributed to the volume of essays on *Woman's Work and Woman's Culture,* published in 1869, reveals the desperation of her reaction to suburban society: the appeal which that chapter embodies for the emancipation of women, " impoverished, deprived of light, hope, instruction and freedom " by virtue of their sex, reads like the cry of a slave or a pauper. It only added to her indignation to find that her neighbours in Sefton Park did not welcome her championship. " Women laying claim for women to certain privileges hitherto withheld " were, she discovered, " called self-seeking and self-asserting—terms applied to them by ladies living at ease, and ignorant of the facts of life, much more frequently than by men ".[50]

Finally, Mrs. Butler was invited to associate herself actively with the campaign by women against the State regulation of prostitution, an invitation which embodied the issues with which she had so long been concerned. Here was the most flagrant of injustices against women, the most outrageous and degrading declaration of their inferiority. Here were men at their most vile. She found herself so shaken by fruitless anger, and even hatred, that she was afraid to make a decision. " I worked hard at other things—good works, as I thought—with a kind of half-conscious hope that God would

[47] *Ibid.,* p. xi.
[48] *Ibid.,* p. xx, footnote.
[49] Johnson, *op. cit.,* chapter 5.
[50] *Woman's Work,* p. xiii.

accept *that* work, and not require me to go further, and run my heart against the naked sword which seemed to be held out ".[51] She recognised that to take up the fight in a spirit of the antagonism of one sex to another would have been disastrous to herself and useless to the cause. She prayed that the emotions of her wounded and revolted heart might be transmuted into a profound hatred of all injustice and cruelty, an anger without sin, tempered with the divine compassion which springs from love. The triumphant issue of this struggle with her baser self sets Josephine Butler far beyond the reach of the analyst. She took the common clay of her emotions and infused them with a divinity of purpose; and in that repellent crusade found at last, not escape from what had been her obsession but its most triumphant use as a weapon against the very evil which had inspired it.

The individual glory of Josephine Butler's life was her own, but the pattern of it was to become increasingly common. More and more women were to find, as she had done, that the path to their own emancipation lay in the service of others who were even more depressed and downtrodden than they were themselves. This capacity to relate their concern for others to their own experience and difficulties was to prove a powerful force in years to come, though at the time its potentialities were not realised. "We know how to manage any other opposition in the House or in the country", a Member of Parliament is reputed to have said of the first petition organised by Josephine Butler, " but it is very awkward for us—this revolt of women. It is quite a new thing; what are we to do with such opposition as this?".[52] The answer to that question nobody could foresee. But from then on, the story of charitable effort was to be intimately bound up with the struggle of countless women to find, and take their place in, the new society of the industrial age.

[51] Johnson, *op. cit.*, p. 90.
[52] Josephine Butler, *Personal Reminiscences of a Great Crusade* (Horace Marshall & Son, 1896), p. 20.

CHAPTER VI

ORGANISED CHARITY: "METHOD VERSUS MUDDLE". 1860-1875.

WILLIAM RATHBONE, writing in 1867, found himself compelled to point out that:—" as a general rule it is no more than the truth that large numbers of the poor of a great town are left to themselves, without protection, without supervision, without help, without recognition from the rich. They belong to no one. There is no one on whom they have an acknowledged claim; . . . . . They fall ill and die, they starve, they suffer, they recover, they find work or lose it, without receiving one word of sympathy, one look of recognition, a helping hand . . . from any man belonging to a social rank above their own."[1] There had in fact always been those who realised that behind the façade of philanthropy lay an agonising inadequacy in the face of a problem of increasing gravity. This feeling gained ground as the century progressed, and in 1868 *Porcupine* openly declared that " pauperism is literally flooding us. It is growing much faster than our growth: strengthening out of all proportion with our strength. Fast as our population increases, the increase of our pauperism is far quicker. It may almost be said that every man earning a living in this town has now a pauper on his back."[2] The very framework of society seemed to be endangered by " the permanent imposition of a whole class for support upon the industrious half of the community ".

The social problems of the 'sixties were a cause of serious alarm to the responsible citizens of the period: briefly put, pauperism was increasing, whilst the means of dealing with it remained static. To meet this grave situation there existed the Poor Law, designed to cater for only a limited number: charity, willy nilly, fell heir to all the rest, regardless of its capacity or inclination.

The fears and anxieties regarding the state of the poor which had been provoked by the events of the 'forties had dulled as the years receded, swamped by the rising materialism of a wholly commercial community. "Has not the love of wealth, the race to be rich at all hazards, led lately to such exhibitions of selfishness and rapacity as have no comparison with any that have gone before? ".[3] In this atmosphere, the spirit of charity languished. Mr. Rathbone publicly denounced the number of people who came to Liverpool to make

[1] *Op. cit.*, p. 52.
[2] *Porcupine*, 30th May, 1868.
[3] Hugh Shimmin. *The Sanitary Aspect of Philanthropy*. An Address delivered to the Y.M.C.A. at the Liverpool College, 12th December, 1865. Published by request, 1866.

81

their fortunes and meanly shrank from the burdens to which the trade and population of the town gave rise.[4] The main burden of charitable work was still borne by a tiny minority whose numbers showed no very great increase on those of forty years ago. "There are people among us who never fail in their Christian duty . . . . but then these generous and energetic persons are not many. They are as nothing when compared with those who do nothing—who never give to any charity—never exert themselves in any good cause. The bulk of the Liverpool public is a solid, inert, almost insoluble mass, not warmed or melted by any impulse or any sunny ray of charity. It does not occur to them to do anything: it does not seem any part of their business. The really beneficent workers of Liverpool are always hot as the three hundred Spartans in the gap—the three Romans on the bridge."[5] So wrote *Porcupine* in an endeavour to sting the public conscience regarding an infant who had died of cold and exposure even though it lay for warmth in bed between its young father and mother.

But though indifferent to *Porcupine's* sarcasm, and to reminders of their social duties uttered by the merchant princes, the public at large could not resist the obtrusion into their personal lives of extreme wretchedness. The cripple in the gutter who displayed his deformity, the beggar who marshalled an imposing array of starving children, the boy who pressed the sale of his "last" newspapers, were sure of a response from passers-by, regardless of whether or not their deformities were bogus, their children borrowed, or their paper-selling a skilful technique. Neither *Porcupine* nor anyone else ever attempted to estimate the amount of charity indiscriminately given by the public, but from the frequency with which the practice was denounced by responsible people the total must have been considerable. In vain the charitable agencies besought the public to restrain their impulse to generosity. As William Rathbone shrewdly perceived : —

"The desultory nature of so much of our charity; the stimulus it requires from fancy balls and bazaars; the greater facility with which a new institution obtains subscriptions for want of which an old one, equally meritorious, languishes; the amount of time and energy which the managers of a charity are so often forced to consume in drumming together the funds required for its support—time and energy which should be devoted to the mere task of efficient management—all these are significant evidence that the manifestations of generosity of which we hear so much proceed not from a strong and clear sense of duty, but from a vague sentiment of compassion; that people give less in obedience to principle than under a sudden

[4] *Porcupine*, 13th January, 1866.
[5] *Ibid*, 9th January, 1867.

impulse of feeling, less to fulfil an obligation than to relieve themselves of an uneasy though vague sense of compunction."[6]

The degeneration of character which followed upon indiscriminate giving was so striking as to dominate serious thinking on social problems for the remainder of the century. Even thoughtful charity came to be suspect, and compassion tended to wither away before the exposure of its possible effects. Yet the attempt to restrict benevolence to responsible channels inevitably drew attention to the fact that the provision these made for the complex wants of the masses of the poor was both inefficient and inadequate. So much so, that *Porcupine* openly declared his fear that the day of voluntary charity was done.[7]

The charitable services had originated in the reaction of individuals to specific situations rather than in methodical planning, with the result that the work of some societies overlapped whilst there were gaps where no provision at all was made. Co-operation between the various societies was sadly lacking, and the consequent competition amongst them for subscriptions caused what *Porcupine* aptly called "trumpet-blowing machinery" to become most undesirably common. Money-raising became a matter of skilled technique, and patronage, as witness the proffering of testimonials to leading supporters. "In some cases the prospective recipient is the chief instigator of the movement, in others he is the principal subscriber to the fund. In this instance there were no public meetings, after-dinner subscriptions, application of pressure or of the screw in any form; no heavy advertising accounts, powerful appeals, importunate applications; no leakage to rapacious collectors, who in some instances consider themselves inadequately paid in retaining for their own use principal and commission".[8]

Bogus charities and bogus clients were becoming more frequent: maladministration to the point of outright corruption came between the subscriber and the object of his charity so that the entire income of a society was sometimes consumed in the process, whilst the system of awarding help to nominees of subscribers was particularly open to abuse. The established societies tended to fall into the hands of a clique, pride being taken in the retention of office by a particular family or congregation over a prodigious number of years: "the charities, unfortunately, are managed without system. A few old fogies are put upon the committee, and are considered *gods*; and anyone recommending an improvement is pooh-poohed."[9] This exclusiveness extended to the subscription lists, and in defence of

[6] *Op. cit.*, p. 36.

[7] *e.g.* 1st June, 1867.

[8] Robert Smiles. *Memoir of the Late Henry Booth.* (Wyman and Sons, 1869.) p. 54.

[9] *Porcupine*, 27th January, 1866.

the shop-keeping class it was claimed that they were not even asked to contribute,[10] at least to the more exclusive voluntary societies. Charitable effort was shot through with the current snobbery: three young men were excluded from races run in aid of the Dental Dispensary on the grounds that they were in trade and not in a merchant's office.[11]

The inadequacy of existing charitable effort made it difficult to decide what was the true function of charity in the existing circumstances. *Porcupine* had no doubt that the great social questions involved in sanitary reform, for example, offered to philanthropy only scope for palliation unless it entered into a real partnership with the law; without " the law to aid us, our efforts will be as water spilled upon the ground ". That this carried implications which were contrary to general opinion he was well aware, but he sturdily declared that: " We in Liverpool are disposed to pay such respect to the venerable English Bogie—the liberty of the subject, that we give the people liberty to live in such a condition as to destroy, not simply their own lives and that of their families and neighbours, but seriously to threaten our own. We are disposed in other matters to forget all about the liberty of the subject, and we must cast it aside in matters affecting public health."[12] His suggestion that this argument might apply to the relief of poverty as well as to the reform of public sanitation was not taken seriously. The experience of the Poor Law was proof enough, if proof was required on so obvious a point, of the unsatisfactory result of dealing with the poor by means of a state agency and it was taken for granted that the amelioration of poverty should remain a matter for voluntary action. The method, and not the principle, of charity was the subject of criticism. How to rouse the indifferent to a sense of their obligations, to expose the impostor, to safeguard the deserving poor against undiscriminating doles; these were the matters which called for reform. But by whom?

As agencies for ameliorating the condition of the poor, the churches were at a disadvantage. The Catholic priests inherited their traditional prestige amongst the Irish but Dissenter and Anglican alike were viewed with antagonism as representatives of the respectable. Whatever his denomination, it took a brave man, and one unusually determined in his faith, to face the difficulties of a ministry to the poor. The Rev. A. Hume, who was active in drawing public attention to the state of the church in poor parishes describes how the Minister in a poor parish stood almost alone, surrounded by " the helpless and hopeless: the poor whom he cannot relieve, the vicious whom he cannot improve, the ignorant whom he cannot

---

[10] *Ibid.*, 1st January, 1865.
[11] *Ibid.*, 22nd August, 1863.
[12] Shimmin, *op. cit.*

enlighten, the ungodly whom he cannot convince. At the same time, he is looked upon by many of the poor, not as a minister of the Gospel, but as a peculiar kind of relieving officer. They never apply to him for spiritual consolation, but they believe that he is morally indebted to them, at least sixpence or a shilling each, for every time that they make their appearance in his Church "[13]

The extent to which practical charity ought to be undertaken by religious bodies presented an even more difficult question. Some continued the habit of material almsgiving long after the administration of the Poor Law had been secularised, and the Society of St. Vincent de Paul is an outstanding example of a body which came into existence for the specific purpose of demonstrating the practical application of Christianity to the problems of poverty.[14]

On the other hand, Thom found many supporters when, on his return to Renshaw Street after three years of retirement for contemplation, he gave it as his considered opinion that "in point of fact, the schemes of philanthropy that characterise this age are not in the hands of the professional servants of religion. That they are not is among the best signs of these times. . . . A Christian Church is not a society for the administration of material charity. Everything it does in this way should be of an incidental and occasional nature. It deals primarily in light for the soul, strength for the character, sympathy for the higher affections, not in alms for the body ".[15] It would convey a false impression of a man of exceptional social sensibility to omit to add that Thom's whole case was based on the argument that benevolence was not a prerogative of the clergy: it was for the preacher to instigate and suggest, for "with the layman, as is natural, is deposited the larger measure of ability to execute the projects to which the Preacher points ".[16] Thom had suggested "many years ago "[17] a Congregational Constitution which would incorporate its social and welfare agencies into the fabric of the church, but had failed to secure support for the scheme. Source of inspiration though he proved to be, he was not strong enough to stand out against a tide which had set so strongly and his own church displayed as much as any other that "contraction of territory within which the writ of religion was conceived to run ".[18]

[13] Abraham Hume. *Missions at Home, or a Clergyman's Account of a Portion of the Town of Liverpool,* 1850.
[14] Society of St. Vincent de Paul, Liverpool Central Council, 1947. Annual Report, including Report of Centenary Celebrations.
[15] *The Preacher and the Church.* Three Sermons preached to the Congregation of Renshaw Street Chapel, Liverpool, November 1857, on resuming his ministry at that place. John Hamilton Thom (Whitfield 1857). pp. 14 & 45.
[16] *Ibid.,* p. 14.
[17] *Ibid.,* p. 35.
[18] R. H. Tawney. *Religion and the Rise of Capitalism.* (Pelican Books, 1938.) p. 246.

It is significant that from this period dates the cleavage between the business world and the religious which was in such contrast to the happy combination of the two characteristic of earlier years. The clergyman, the missioner, the Bible reader, were respected in their own sphere, but the value of their contribution to the practical problems of poverty was held to be negligible. In addition, intellectual interest had shifted from the philosophical to the political and economic. It is therefore not surprising to find that the lead in the movement for the reform of charitable effort was taken by a business man, and that his contribution consisted of the application of principles of business method to the muddle of charitable work.

William Rathbone cannot be viewed other than as a member of his family. His daughter wrote of him that, " it was impossible not to feel to how unusual an extent [his] life and character were the outcome and the natural continuation of the lives that had gone before. But for the incidents of birth and death, they might seem at least on a cursory view which ignored the real differences of individuality and power to be but a single life extended over three generations ".[19]

William Rathbone's mother belonged to the equally eminent Greg family[20] of Quarry Bank, near Manchester. " . . . Between her and her eldest son, William, there was a very strong resemblance —physical, mental, moral. Both had an abounding, exuberant, extraordinarily tenacious vitality. The bent of both minds was intensely practical, amounting almost to the genius of commonsense. In both, at least in their old age, conscience and will seemed almost to have grown into one; so that what they felt to be right, that they instinctively wished, and desired, and strove at once to do."[21] His father took a prominent part in local affairs, and was the first nonconformist Mayor of Liverpool, but it was to his mother that he owed that personal acquaintance with the condition of the poor which became one of his most useful assets.

"His venerated mother had devoted much of her time and thought to the welfare of the poor, and had been, if not the originator, one of the most energetic friends of that truly noble and useful society, the Liverpool Domestic Mission. In connection with this their son, then a wealthy and carefully nurtured youth, had become personally familiar with the household life of the 'great residuum'. When a mere lad he had accompanied her in her visits

[19] E. Rathbone, *op. cit.,* p. 53.

[20] The Greg family were Unitarians, and as the fifth William Rathbone was then a Quaker, his marriage with Elizabeth Greg was not approved by the Society. It was four years after the birth of their son, William, that they finally severed their connection with the Society and joined a congregation of Unitarians.

[21] E. Rathbone, *op. cit.* p. 40.

to the poor. He had seen her originate a scheme from which after-wards arose the Corporation Wash-houses; and another by which, long before cheap, free News Rooms were widely known or even projected, she enabled her humble friends to read the papers and obtain useful books. And when she had passed away, he took up her mantle, went on with her projects, and did what, though unostentatiously performed, was laborious, self-sacrificing, fre-quently most unpleasant work."[22]

The only suggestion that William Rathbone ever seriously wavered in his acceptance of the family tradition occurs in his account of the emotion with which he heard Thom's appeal for a Special Mission to the Poor.

"He called on us to consider what the Christianity of our age was worth, and told us that what we as Christians are is to be seen in what those who live by the people and wield the influences of society suffer the people to be. I was just then entering on the world's work, with all the hopes and aspirations of seventeen, and I felt so strongly the truth of the preacher's words that had I not doubted my power of influencing others by speech—I believe I should have abandoned the desk for work in the streets and courts of our town."[23]

What that decision cost him is not known, beyond the fact that years later he asserted his conviction that to have been successful in preaching the gospel to the poor would have far outweighed any-thing he actually achieved. As it was, viewing the issue in the light of commonsense, he decided that for him, an effective life of public service would depend on his possession of the influence and respect secured by success in business. Accordingly, he set himself doggedly to the task of building up the family fortunes which had suffered from the devotion of his father and grandfather to public work.

This might well have seen the end of his interest in the poor. As he himself observed, increasing wealth was all too apt to bring about in its owner a hardening or pecuniary paralysis, and neglect of public duty. This was unlikely to befall any member of that family of habitual philanthropists, but in William Rathbone's case, to inherited tradition was added the unquenchable inspiration of the teaching of John Hamilton Thom. To one reared in an atmosphere where no distinction was permitted between precept and practice, Thom's vision of Christianity as a practical way of life made an instant appeal, and it was to Thom that William Rathbone freely expressed himself as indebted for the inspiration of his charity.

For some years, his concentration on business affairs was apparently complete, though one of his first actions on entering his

[22] B. G. Orchard. *Second Series of the Liverpool Exchange Portrait Gallery*. (Privately printed, 1884.) p. 68.
[23] E. Rathbone, *op. cit.*, p. 70.

father's office was to persuade him to send all the beggars who hung about its doors to a charitable agency for investigation before awarding them alms.[24] However, the acute awareness of "unsuspected obligations" fostered by his association with Thom, who became his brother-in-law in 1838, kept alive the impression made upon him by his mother's charitable work. In 1849, he undertook responsibility for a district of the District Provident Society,[25] and a few years later, no doubt caught up by the "fashion for philanthropy" of that time, he seems to have agreed with his father that he should devote more time to public work. He was soon involved in a situation which demonstrated to him the need for applying to charitable administration those principles on which he had early resolved to conduct his own affairs. The account of this is worth quoting since it bears evidence of having been written by Mr. Rathbone himself.

"... In the Spring of 1855, when imports by steamers were of comparatively small amount, a long succession of east winds, and consequent delay in the arrival of vessels, kept many hundreds of men without employment, causing great distress amongst the labouring population. This was much intensified by a long continuance of frost which threw masons, brick-layers, and others connected with the building and out-door trades, also out of work. The large number of men standing about the Exchange, waiting for the chance of employment, attracted the attention of some of the leading philanthropists of the town, and led them to start a fund for the relief more immediately of porters, though it soon widened, and covered a more general and extensive area.

The plan adopted by a Distribution Committee which was formed was to allot tickets representing a specified amount of relief amongst the employers of labour. This might have worked well enough as regards men generally working for one employer, but the great bulk of applicants had only occasional work from different employers, and the consequence was that the designing got tickets from all, and great abuse was the natural result.

About £5,000 was raised and distributed in about six weeks, and, as one closely connected with the movement afterwards said £10,000 worth of harm was done.

At that time there were in operation in Liverpool three general relief societies—the District Provident and Strangers' Friend, and the Charitable Society—their relief being principally confined to winter. There was, however, no co-operation or joint action between them, and much abuse of charity resulted in consequence.

[24] See p. 29.

[25] In which work he was outstandingly successful, his total of £198 personally collected being the highest for any voluntary worker at the Domestic Mission Branch of the Society for the year 1852.

This state of things was not improved by the results of the experiment just named. The lesson learnt in 1855 was not lost on recipients of charity, who found that by a little manipulation, relief could be obtained from all three societies at once, there being no exchange of information amongst them. This was abundantly shewn subsequently, when, in several instances, three recommendation notes—one of each society—came forward in favour of the same person at the same time.

Good no doubt came out of evil in this case, for the committees and officers of the three societies were gradually brought to the conclusion that they were being imposed upon; and in the interests of the poor, as well as the rich, were ready to entertain a proposal to amalgamate the three into one."[26]

The conclusions at which he thus arrived as to the importance of method in charitable work, Mr. Rathbone was able to test a few years later when the death of his wife in 1859 stimulated him to found the District Nursing Service.[27] The training of nurses for that scheme led him to membership of the managing body of the Royal Infirmary: experience in charge of a District made him take up the reform of workhouse nursing which, starting with the appointment of Agnes Jones[28] as matron of the hospital wards at the Brownlow Hill Workhouse, eventually influenced the care of the sick pauper throughout the country. The whole question of poor relief interested him and he served on the Select Vestry at a time when this was regarded as no great honour.

In 1867[29] he summed up his conclusions in regard to charity in a small book which he originally called *Method versus Muddle in Charitable Work* though he accepted the advice of a literary friend in publishing it under the title of *Social Duties, considered in Reference to the Organisation of Effort in Works of Benevolence and Public Utility.*[30] Here are enumerated those principles of social obligation upon which his own life and the use of his wealth were based, reduced to terms of the utmost commonsense and practicability. The equality of socialism not appearing to him a practical possibility, his attention centred instead upon the importance of persuading the wealthy to give their minds to the proper, and in the long run the most profitable use of their wealth. Given a change of

[26] *The Elberfeld System of Poor Relief,* as applied in various German Towns. Report of an Inquiry by Aug. F. Hanewinkel, with an introductory sketch of the Society, 1887.

[27] See p. 70 *et seq.*

[28] See p. 76.

[29] In which year, incidentally, the President of the Poor Law Board appealed for an effort to be made to clear up the existing state of confusion in regard to the boundary between public and voluntary relief services.

[30] By a Man of Business. (Macmillan & Co., 1867.)

heart on the part of the prosperous, and a judicious organisation of their benevolence towards the poor, he was convinced that the social strains and resentments which had accompanied the industrial revolution could be remedied. In effect, he advocated a system of voluntary socialism: the rich were voluntarily to limit their personal enjoyment of wealth, and voluntarily to devote their leisure time to administering the surplus on behalf of others.

The contemporary situation thus seemed to him to call for a twofold effort: to rouse the rich to a sense of their social duties, and to work out sound methods whereby they could express their obligations. The former he took to be primarily the duty of the churches, the latter the task which he and his fellow business-men must undertake. He outlined the machinery whereby this last might be achieved, his whole emphasis being laid on the need for reason rather than emotion in charitable work: unless relief was based on a thorough understanding of the circumstances of each individual case, it was more likely to do harm than good. Nevertheless he stipulated that such charity must be based on voluntary service to prevent its becoming harsh and unlovely.

Unfortunately he was never to have the opportunity for himself putting his plan into operation. His election as a Member of Parliament in 1868 inevitably reduced his opportunities for playing an active part in local charitable effort and he became more and more the philanthropist, increasingly absorbed in the discharge of the obligations of wealth and prestige. As such, his influence on Liverpool and, indeed, on national life, was considerable, but his share in the day-to-day administration of charity was limited. A second marriage, family responsibilities centring on the pleasant home at Greenbank, prominence in the movement for the provision of university education in Liverpool and in North Wales, went to make up a life of unparalleled usefulness. William Rathbone died in 1902, at the age of eighty-three, publicly esteemed and lamented as were few men even in those days of lush mourning.

It is difficult to reduce to human proportions the monument of virtue which public regard has made of William Rathbone, all the more so because his habit of anonymity has almost obscured all traces of the "warm and marrowy force of character" which he inherited from his father.[31] Yet the man was no mere monument. There was a glow about him, a vitality and warmth which "had all the effect of opening a window and letting in air and sunshine upon a stuffy room. His very appearance on the platform, his eager look, and the ring in his voice, recalled the slumbering audience to a consciousness of the vital human needs that lay behind the dull mechanism of charity or thrift"[32]

[31] *Porcupine*, 8th June, 1867.
[32] E. Rathbone, *op. cit.*, p. 396.

It is curious that the legacy of so warm-hearted a human being should have been to rid the relationship with the poor of emotion and sentiment. William Rathbone inspired a new method of charity to take the place in the urban community of the neighbourly kindness of previous years, but though he realised the importance of basing this method on a right human relationship, further than this he could not go. He yearned to see a passion of exertion and self-sacrifice flood those who professed to be Christians, and lamented that the figure of twenty thousand voluntary workers for the Central Relief Society's scheme should be regarded as ridiculous: "What a comment on our Christianity!" He cried out for the leadership of "some one or more men of eloquence, and moral power", feeling intense discontent with himself and the class of educated men above the pinch of poverty.[33] Yet it never seems to have occurred to him that this same quality of passion must be extended from the duty to the poor to the actual poor themselves. Indeed, his public life was one long demonstration of a conception of charity from which all sentiment was excluded on principle.[34] Duty and obligation were the cold words with which he appealed to the rich to consider the state of the poor. The lesson which Johns had died in demonstrating and which his own District Nurses could have taught him, that the only footing on which to approach the poor was that of the humility of a servant and not the "charity" of a patron,[35] he could not learn because his reason refused its sense. To him "the people" to whose welfare he dedicated his life, were never to include himself or his like; the working man, however commendable, however admirable, was never to be taken into the bosom of his family, never loved in life nor garlanded with white camellias in death.[36] Looking back on life, he recognised, though still without comprehending, that herein lay the seeds of failure.

"It has always appeared to me that our greatest failure as a Church was the failure to reach and come into personal contact with the great mass of the people from among whom Christ and the first Christians came, and among whom, unhardened by ease and self-indulgence it was most welcome."[37]

[33] *Ibid.*, p. 278.
[34] The sole exception to this rule was the giving of gratuities on departure from foreign hotels, when, his daughter tells us, "he would stand at the door fingering loose coin, and exhorting his party to notice 'whether there was not someone else who looked as if they expected something'." (E. Rathbone, *op. cit.*, p. 130.)
[35] See for instance, Dr. Shadwell, *District Nursing as a Factor in Social Work*. Proceedings. Jubilee Congress of District Nursing, Liverpool. 1909.
[36] Johnson, *op. cit.*, p. 64.
[37] Letter to the Secretary of Congregation (Renshaw Street Chapel) by William Rathbone, April 14th, 1894. Quoted in Anne Holt, *Walking Together*. (George Allen & Unwin, 1938.) p. 231.

In estimating the importance of William Rathbone's effort to introduce method into the muddle of charity, it is important to recollect that it was intended to remedy a special situation. The stirring conscience of the middle classes had given rise to a relationship with the poor which provoked the more thoughtful to the "belief—it may almost be called an obsession—that the mass-misery of great cities arose mainly, if not entirely, from spasmodic, indiscriminate and unconditional doles, whether in the form of alms or that of Poor Law Relief ".[38] In demonstrating how an urban community could express its sense of obligation towards its less fortunate members without detriment to the self-respect of either, William Rathbone made an outstanding contribution to the mechanics of modern social life. To write thus is not to belittle the great good that he did, but to lament that he was not able to add to it the revelation of the means by which the social justice he sought to ensure might be infused with the mercy of charity.

Had he remained in Liverpool to put his theories into practice, William Rathbone might have become aware of the dangers of undue emphasis upon method in relief work. Unfortunately, it was left to others to carry out his intentions, and it is therefore in terms of the Central Relief Society that the story of what became known as organised charity has to be continued.

The efforts to introduce some sort of order into the administration of charitable relief by the amalgamation of the leading societies after the bad Spring of 1855[39] had received a further impetus from the distress caused by the Lancashire Cotton Famine in 1862.

" The amalgamation was carried into effect in January 1863, with the co-operation of the Managers of the three Societies, representatives of all three being included in the Committee of the new Society.

The object which the Central Relief Society thus established had in view at that time was to provide necessaries—chiefly food and fuel—for such deserving families as might from sickness, lack of work, or other temporary cause, be in need of help, and so save them from the necessity of applying for parish relief, when by a few weeks' assistance they might be tided over the emergency."[40]

The objects of the Society as thus presented, are eminently straightforward: a business community faced with such a situation as now obtained in Liverpool could hardly be expected to do otherwise. Indiscriminate charity had borne fruit which could only be regarded with alarm: mendicity had reached proportions which demanded measures of the utmost severity: depravity and degeneration concealed cases of true hardship such as no civilised community

---

[38] Beatrice Webb. *My Apprenticeship.* (Pelican Books, 1938.) p. 227.
[39] See p. 88.
[40] *The Elberfeld System of Poor Relief, op. cit.*

could possibly countenance. Knowing the end of the story, it is easy to belittle its beginning, but the situation was difficult and the philanthropic undeniably tackled it with the same vigour and sincerity as they were accustomed to apply to the pursuit of their own fortunes. Yet it was in precisely this, which they regarded as their virtue, that the source of future trouble lay.

The aim of the Society was little above that of the Poor Law though stress was laid on the importance of not providing a substitute for public assistance. Except in very special instances only the deserving poor in temporary distress were to be assisted, and each application was to be subjected to careful investigation by the paid agents of the Society. The general public was urged to cease from giving money to individuals, and instead to refer both their alms giving and their hard cases to the Society. Relief normally consisted mainly of tickets for soup, bread and groceries, but the Soup Kitchens, which were first placed under the care of the Society and then given to them outright, were intended to assist the working class in general by providing them with opportunities for buying food cheaply, and the public were advised to give soup tickets rather than money, if give they must. The then uncommon practice of granting aid to cover periods of convalescence after sickness was also adopted, doubtless under Mr. Rathbone's influence.

The first Annual Report expressed the Committee's satisfaction with the results of the application of method to the administration of relief: "Your Committee have every reason to report favourably of the operations of the Society; it has not only been successful in relieving a large amount of distress amongst our poorer townsmen, 12,654 cases having been visited, of which 10,511 were relieved, at an expense of £1,414 10s. 5d., an average of 2s. 8d. each, the amount of relief being varied according to circumstances, but it has been the means of exposing the nefarious practices of those who made a business of mendicity, and the stream of charity which is every ready to flow in the direction of really deserving objects has, there is reason to believe, been materially protected from being diverted into an opposite channel. . ."[41] Even so, the Annual Reports contain a regular reminder from then onwards, that the object of the Society is as much to detect as to relieve, and the general public was regrettably slower than the impostors to realise the significance of the Society's existence.

The comparatively large sums spent on administration were held to be justified by the increased efficiency of the service rendered, to which the admirable degree of co-operation between the parish authorities, the District Nurses and the Central Relief Society during the outbreak of cholera in 1865-6 bore witness. The original Slater

[41] C.R.S. Annual Report for 1863-4.

Street scheme[42] for co-ordinating charitable effort had apparently been taken over by the "religious clique", and suggestions of co-operation amongst the charitable agencies met with a poor response. Schemes for the joint collection of subscriptions were put forward in 1856 and 1869, but neither was successful.

Yet though the machinery was improved, the human material with which it was intended to deal remained disappointingly impervious to organisation. The rich continued to ignore their social obligations, and when they did give, to give indiscriminately. The poor were even less responsive; their classification into deserving and undeserving presented unexpected difficulties, and the Society found itself constantly arguing with indignant subscribers as to the correct interpretation of these terms. Moreover, the material relief which it was the Society's main object to organize, proved all too seldom to be the answer to the problem of poverty, whilst self-help was difficult to foster in a world where the ladders up from poverty were so cumbered with obstacles insurmountable by mere virtue and industry. The history of the Society quickly became, in fact, a tug of war between theory and practice, moral precept and economic possibility. Instead of the straightforward job of directing the blessings of charity towards appropriate sheep amongst the poor, leaving the goats to the harsher ministrations of the Poor Law, the Society found itself edged into fields of social experiment far beyond the accepted sphere of philanthropy. As business men, the Committee were quick to realise that the problem of poverty was less a matter for charity than a question of "providing some profitable occupation for the unemployed poor of our large towns—a difficulty which forces itself more urgently upon our attention year by year—each winter bringing with it the same tale of unmitigated, if not increased, distress amongst the working classes".[43] Accordingly in 1869, the rules were altered in order to permit them to accept responsibility for an experimental Fire Lighter Factory which would enable them to offer work to applicants for relief, and at the same time, test their willingness to work. The Committee entertained the strongest conviction that by such means, an opportunity for self-help would be presented to the industrious workman which would do more to promote self-respect and moral elevation than any charitable assistance. They noted that incidentally, "in an economical point of view the result would be beneficial to the Society, in as much as the amount of money paid in wages would be partly compensated by a diminution of the amount directly expended in relief".[44]

The Committee struggled to realise the theoretical independence

[42] See p. 28.
[43] C.R.S. Annual Report, 1869.
[44] *Ibid.*

of the scheme, but they were too shrewd to continue indefinitely to soak up the surplus of the labour market with the blotting paper of charity, and shortly concluded that the factory must be evaluated from the point of view of philanthropy and not of economics, the real cause of the trouble being an excess of labour. A scheme for assisted migration to manufacturing districts, primarily of widows with children, was also operated, but the number of satisfactory cases remained small in proportion to the trouble involved.

However, the main work of the Society remained the giving of relief to persons in temporary distress, involving annual sums of three or four thousand pounds, and much anxious thought lest further pauperisation be the main result. The publication of statistical records revealed a steady increase in the amount of work undertaken, but the Society viewed this as wholly satisfactory, and remained confident that if only the public would increase their support of organised charity, and the charitable societies practice co-operation, the problem of aiding the deserving poor would be solved.

The Annual Reports on all this activity read as what in fact they were, business-like accounts rendered to shareholders of transactions concluded on their behalf. The state of trade with some reference to the weather is discussed as the determining factor in the amount of work done by the Society, and supporters are asked to give, not according to their capacity, but according to the demand as thus forecast. So many cases are reported as having been investigated, so many rejected, so many relieved. On the record goes, with never a word of pity for the anguish of a bitter winter, never a sigh for the fate of those sent empty away. This was, of course, a matter of deliberate policy: the whole purpose of the scheme was to put charity on a businesslike footing. Only if dispensed with the impartiality of justice could charity avoid bringing in its train the very degeneration of character which it was designed to check. Whether justice and charity could walk hand in hand, however, remained to be seen. The Central Relief Society met the distressing discrepancy between the thousand and more men offered work at the Firelighter Factory and the 450 who acepted it, with the firm statement that this only went to show how numerous were the undeserving. Mr. Rathbone's plea for basing the administration of charity upon the human relations between individual rich and poor was apparenuy forgotten, and the conviction gained ground that the task of organised charity must be to organise still better, to enquire even more diligently. How otherwise to prevent " even well-to-do artisans and mechanics "[45] from leaning yet more heavily upon the beneficence of charitable institutions?

Yet this was precisely what was already earning them the reputa-

[45] C.R.S. Annual Report, 1883.

tion of being even harsher than the Poor Law, so that the poor suffered in silence sooner than bear the indignity of the Society's investigation into their affairs, and the kindly preferred to run the risk of being deceived rather than submit their poor friends to an exposure which they themselves would bitterly have resented. In spite of their protestations, the Society had, in fact, created a service remarkably like that of the Poor Law, and the original virtue which had been claimed for the Society in that it was a voluntary and not a State agency, had been lost sight of.

The technique of " case-work " has become such an accepted feature of the landscape of the social services that it is difficult to grasp the degree of opposition which it originally aroused. The fact that the Annual Meetings of the Society were frequently made the occasion of stout denials of charges of harshness and inhumanity demonstrates the reality of the resentment felt towards the Society's methods. Many of the churches refused to submit their endeavours to organisation by the Central Relief Society. The relief of the poor they admitted to be a thorny problem, but nevertheless their workers were exhorted not to hand on cases to the Society whose visitors " oftentimes excel the Relieving Officers in their unnecessarily painful enquiries: besides to shirk this duty, would be an imperfect following of the Lord Jesus Christ who attended to the *bodies* as well as to the *souls* of men ".[46] The clergy of all denominations, as might be expected, provided outstanding examples of this attitude, and if Canon Lester is quoted in preference to others, it is only because the work he did and the way he did it provide a particularly apt illustration of all that was typical of those who, consciously or unconsciously, opposed the principles of organised charity.

The early influence of F. D. Maurice on the life of Major Lester[47] made it inevitable that on arrival as a young clergyman in the Kirkdale district of Liverpool in 1853, he should feel impelled to do more than preach to the ill-fed and uncared for people of his overcrowded parish. Goaded by the inadequacy of work in a Ragged Mission Room over a coal-shed, he eventually embarked on the Kirkdale Child Charity with which his name was always associated. In this, his aim was no less than to feed, clothe and train for a trade, any child whatsoever, regardless of denomination or indeed of anything else except the fact of immediate distress. Starting modestly, this inevitably became a stupendous task, especially as there was then only one other school for that whole population of nine thousand. The Canon was forced to devote himself to begging for money, for which he developed a remarkable technique, personally raising as much as four thousand pounds a year. Once he broke down under

[46] Postance, *op. cit.*
[47] Rev. A. H. Edwards, M.A. *A Great Heart.* (Nisbet, 1906.)

the strain, and his bitterness in later years over the failure of the public to give his work even greater support shook Lee Jones[48] when as a young man he called upon the then elderly Canon for advice. Even the children were used to exploit sentiment in their own support, and their efforts with Child Charity Boxes became almost a public nuisance. The boys fetched broken meats from the dining saloons of ships in port, the girls turned out between two and three thousand paper bags daily. The boys' brass band inevitable to every such institution simultaneously earned money and attracted useful publicity.

Canon Lester became known as a great fighter on behalf of the poor, and for this reason was commonly called "The Major", although the name was in fact a family one. He was widely respected and admired, serving as Chairman of the Liverpool Education Board for a time, and when he died in 1903 his schools were officially named after him as a public tribute. Yet for all his popularity, for all the esteem in which his work was held, the Homes to which he had devoted his life had to be shut for lack of support after his death, and the schools handed over to the local education authority. Against the apparent failure of his charity to achieve permanence must, however, be set the fact that he so triumphantly convinced the poor of his sincerity: the genuine affection with which he was regarded by them lives on in the hearts of succeeding generations.[49] To the hopeless and helpless, the material benefits which he secured for their children were tangible evidence of his deep concern for their well-being, a concern which they experienced all too seldom.

William Rathbone had demanded, and rightly so, that in justice to the poor, the methods of charity should be subjected to reason. Major Lester stood for a reminder of the fundamental faith that the "spirit of unquestioning, of unrestricted—in short, of infinite—charity was, to the orthodox Christian, not a process by which a given end could be attained, but an end in itself—a state of mind—one of the main channels through which the individual entered into communion with the supreme spirit of love at work in the universe".[50] The infusion of the method of the one by the spirit of the other was essential to the evolution of satisfactory human relationships in the new industrial society. This was the task which remained to be done, and the resolution of the apparent conflict between the two types of approach was to underlie the charitable work of the rest of the century.

[48] See p. 119 *et seq*.
[49] The classic anecdote about him records the reply of a local woman to the Major's comment on the enormous turn-out to see his daughter married. "But just think", she said, "what it will be like at your own funeral".
[50] Webb, *op. cit.*, p. 225.

CHAPTER VII

THE GREAT DEPRESSION: "PERSONAL SERVICE" 1875-1890

THE contrast presented by the extremes of wealth and poverty which had long characterised the town, was now sharpened by the prevalence of a more blatant materialism than had ever been known before. The Rev. Acland Armstrong wrote of his first impression on arriving in Liverpool in 1884 to take up work as minister to the Unitarian congregation at Hope Street:

"I came to Liverpool a stranger some six or seven years ago, knowing only that I was about to take up my residence in the second city of the mightiest Empire the world has ever seen. I admired its public buildings, its vast docks, its stately shipping, its splendid shops, its lovely parks. It seemed to me that this was a city in which one might be proud to be a citizen; a city which must be administered and governed by men of high capacity and generous temper.

"But after the first glance I was appalled by one aspect of things here which pressed in upon my mind more and more for several weeks, till the sin of it became at times well nigh unbearable. The contiguity of immense wealth and abysmal poverty forced itself upon my notice. The hordes of the ragged and the wretched surged up from their native quarters and covered the noblest streets like a flood. Men and women in the cruellest grip of poverty, little children with shoeless feet, bodies pinched and faces in which the pure light of childhood had been quenched, swarmed on the very pavements that fronted the most brilliant shops; and the superb carriages of the rich, with their freights of refined and elegant ladies, threaded their way among sections of the population so miserable and squalid that my heart ached at the sight of them. I had seen wealth. I had seen poverty. But never before had I seen the two so jammed together. Never before had I seen streets, loaded with all that wealth can buy, lined with the haunts of hopeless penury. I knew that there were great Christian charities in Liverpool. I knew that there were men and women holding their wealth a trust from God. But soon it was irresistibly impressed upon me that in the mass the wealth cared little for the poverty and the squalor, but it took its ease or ran the race for riches with heart unstirred by the terrible poverty of tens of thousands, and conscience unawakened to the tremendous responsibilities which wealth entails".[1]

The example of the rich infected the whole life of the city, so

[1] Richard Acland Armstrong. *The Deadly Shame of Liverpool.* 1890.

that indifference to social responsibilities characterized every class.[2] The vested interests of the breweries, together with the shocking housing situation, and the lack of steady employment, stalemated every effort of the philanthropic to deal constructively with the wretchedness of the poor. Their sense of helplessness was added to by the indifferent giving of the wealthy, and the tendency of the working-classes to lean upon charity sooner than struggle for independence. The comment of the *Liverpool Daily Post* on the state of public health might well have been applied to public morals and social conditions in general: " Liverpool has throughout the last forty years stood, as she stands today, supreme in the black list: —

" By merit raised
To that bad eminence "[3]

Against such a weight of indifference, charitable effort could make little headway. Indeed, the established societies were themselves invaded by a commercial spirit, and a surgeon wrote to *Porcupine* complaining of " the eager competition among the committees of various charities for *numbers* of patients. They do not care who apply, so long as they go in numbers, that a great front may be shown, and a larger share of the funds appropriated to their benefit. The result has been extremely detrimental to all classes. The spirit of independence formerly so characteristic of the British man and woman is fast going, and, in its place a disposition to lean on charity is becoming paramount."[4]

Every effort to interest the general public in their charitable duty seemed doomed to failure till in 1883, the outstanding success of *The Bitter Cry of Outcast London* inspired the *Liverpool Daily Post* to publish a similar description of the state of the local poor. A special Commission consisting of a City Councillor, a prominent local physician, and a member of their own staff, was asked to report on conditions in the poorest quarters, " in the hope of arousing the inhabitants of Liverpool to a sense of the seriousness of the existing situation and of the imperativeness of their duty towards a huge population which lives at their very doors under conditions of life so horrible as to well nigh defy description."[5]

---

[2] A survey made in 1873 revealed the limited extent to which the burden of charity was shared amongst the community. It was estimated that of a total of 20,000 possible contributors, only 6,688 actually contributed, of whom 1,193 provided considerably more than half of the total sum. A strongly supported memorial was sent to the Mayor asking him to promote the opening of a central office for joint collection by the main societies. This failed to materialise, though in 1877 the Central Relief Society managed to persuade 18 societies to permit it to act as their collector during the first two months of the year. (W. Grisewood. *The Collection of Subscriptions.* 1906.)

[3] *Liverpool Daily Post,* 2nd November, 1883.
[4] *Porcupine,* 13th March, 1880.
[5] *Liverpool Daily Post,* 5th November, 1883.

The Commission reported in a series of lurid articles, entitled
Squalid Liverpool, which gain perhaps their greatest horror from
their very repetition of what Shimmin had written so many years
earlier. It seemed as if all the patient effort of sanitary reform had
been unable even to hold its own against the downward drag of sheer
numbers. " Houses are not like wine or cheese—they do not improve
by keeping," Shimmin had said[6] and many of the houses of which he
said it were still standing, crammed to the roof with wretched
humanity. *Squalid Liverpool* described, street by street, the foundations of human misery upon which the life of the city was built, the
shocked horror of the Commissioners at the proximity of such
poverty to the wealth of the city underlining every word they wrote.
Of a district off Scotland Road, for example, they said :

" It is as dirty, as tumble-down, and as unhealthy as any portion
of squalid Liverpool, and it lies within a stone's-throw of prosperous,
money-making Liverpool—the Liverpool of clubs, of *cafes,* of
banks, of commercial palaces. Walk along Dale Street as the sun
glistens on the shop windows, throwing the shadow of the lofty spire
of the Municipal Offices like the pointer of a huge sun-dial across
the street; as gossiping politicians lounge on the steps of the Reform
Club and the Conservative Club; as carriages rattle along, convey-
ing wealthy merchants from splendid offices to suburban halls; you
find traces wherever your eye turns of wealth and ambition—
political, municipal, and commercial—of busy, happy men, all bent
upon winning some prize in the world, and you might easily imagine
that no dark shade of squalor rested upon the broad face of Liverpool. Yet walk a few paces from this bright and cheering scene, and
you will find gathered upon the very edge of it a deep fringe of
suffering, helpless, hopeless poverty, all the more distressing in that
it is so near a region of hope, of comfort, and of activity."[7]

The Commissioners, by virtue of their respective callings, were
already familiar with the facts of poverty, but their investigations
" revealed to them a depth of distress, of sin, and of suffering of
which they before had formed no conception. The object of these
articles has been to describe, and not prescribe. But your Commissioners are profoundly impressed with the necessity for swift and
strong action. Neglect has bred a multitude of dangers, and the
number is increasing every day. The welfare of society demands
that this matter of the housing of the poor shall be trifled with no
longer ".

The Commissioners were themselves shocked and alarmed by
their findings, but the public reaction must nevertheless have come
as something of a surprise. The articles had to be reprinted in

---

[6] *Sanitary Aspect of Philanthropy, op. cit.*
[7] *Squalid Liverpool,* (Reprinted from *The Liverpool Daily Post,* 1883), p. 35.

pamphlet form to meet the demand. Lectures, letters to the press, talks and sermons, and organised visits to the poor followed in profusion. Even the most conservative of rate-payers joined in the demand that something should be done about the poor. " Unless the public assert themselves, these people will be permitted to sink to deeper depths, until some frightful epidemic breaks out and clears us all away, simple and gentle, in common ruin. The only chance of averting such a horrible calamity is by bringing before the eyes of the inhabitants the wens, blisters, and sores of the city, and stirring up the manly sympathies of the public."[8]

Squalid Liverpool was an effective piece of writing, but some further explanation is required to account for its success in catching public attention where so many previous endeavours had failed. The truth was that the depressions of 1875 and the following years had insidiously undermined the faith in economic liberalism which alone justified the attitude to poverty as the inevitable reward of individual lack of merit. There had been depressions before. Liverpool's dependence on its fortunes as a port rendered it specially sensitive to the vagaries of wind, weather and the international situation, but the sense of depression which encompassed the middle classes in the late seventies and the following decade[9] sprang from causes at once more permanent and more profound than a wind from the east or a threat from abroad. For the first time since the industrial boom began, a halt was called to progress : for the first time, it was the security of the middle classes which was threatened.

" It was believed . . . that of all the subscribers [on the Exchange] i.e. such as were in business for themselves, three-fourths of those who had traded for ten years had, in some form or another, failed to meet their engagements."[10] Lower in the social scale, the new insecurity hit even harder. The Liverpool Clerks Association tried desperately to provide relief in the shape of employment for those of its members who were out of work,[11] but were forced to the bitter conclusion that " clerks are the unskilled labourers of the middle classes, and like their brethren of the working classes, have overstocked the market. . . . They are the children of small shopkeepers and better class artisans, who have been consumed by an

---

[8] *The Dwellings of the Industrial Classes in the Diocese of Liverpool and How to Improve Them.* A Paper read at the Liverpool Diocesan Conference by A. B. Forwood, 6th November, 1883.

[9] W. W. Rostov. *Investment and Real Wages.* 1873-86. *Economic History Review,* May, 1939. *Investment and the Great Depression. Economic History Review,* May, 1938.

[10] B. G. Orchard. *Twenty Literary Portraits of Business Men.* First series. (Mathews Bros., 1884).

[11] *Porcupine,* 20th March, 1881.

ambition to wear black coats and be a 'gentleman'. . . . Hosts of them ought never to have been clerks at all ".[12]

This was an experience so rare in their long enjoyment of progress and prosperity as to jolt the middle classes right out of their accustomed ways of thinking, rendering them open to ideas and feelings to which they had previously been impervious. In the first instance their changed attitude was perhaps attributable to fear of physical infection, to which recent advances in medical knowledge largely contributed. The Medical Officer of Health wrote that " There is a large and growing class among us who almost appear to be beyond the pale of enlightenment—they are left to themselves and forgotten; but disease, fostered by their habits, is apt to break through the boundaries of the unhealthy districts, and spread its lethal shadow far and wide. The public should bear in mind that as the strength of a chain is that of its weakest link, so the health of the community is that of its weakest member. And so long as unhealthy areas are allowed to continue, so long will the public health suffer ".[13] However, the immense importance attached to the fact that poverty was a continuing state and not, as hitherto assumed, a temporary incident in life, indicated a reaction to something more profound than fear of merely physical infection. " What is here said by Dr. Taylor of physical health applies equally to moral and spiritual health ", was the comment of the Secretary to the Central Relief Society, a sentiment which Cardinal Manning expressed more forcibly when he said that " it was in great centres like Liverpool that drunkenness had its chief hold, and it was there that the population had become maddened and dangerous, so that at any time a spark might fall, there was ready a heap of combustion ".[14]

This fear demonstrated a most unusual lack of confidence in both themselves and their way of life on the part of the middle classes which was of the utmost importance in its consequences on the attitude towards the problem of poverty. Shaken by the experience of serious economic insecurity, the middle classes regarded any divergence from the accepted code of behaviour, such as the lack of industry, sobriety and thrift amongst the ' poorest of the poor ', as a further threat to the *status quo*. Their immediate reaction was one of moral indignation that the poor should repudiate what they themselves had toiled to maintain. This even extended to those who co-operated in the misbehaviour of the poor by selling them drink, or under-paying them for their labour as match girls or dock labourers, so that the temperance movement, for example, took on

[12] Hugh C. Farrie. *Toiling Liverpool.* (Reprinted from the *Liverpool Daily Post,* 1886), p. 53.

[13] Quoted in *The Relief of the Poor.* A Paper read by William Grisewood at a Conference of the Rural Deanery of Walton, 10th June, 1884.

[14] *Liverpool Daily Post,* 20th June, 1884.

a new lease of life in attacking the brewers and publicans. However, though indignation rather than pity filled the breasts of the upright, the outcome was the same, namely, bewilderment as to how the poor, especially the undeserving, could be inculcated with that zeal for industry and thrift upon which social progress was held to depend, and fear of the consequences of failure to do so. Viewed in this light, orthodox charity, with its emphasis on material relief, and the assistance of the " deserving ", appeared to be quite irrelevant to the necessities of the situation, whilst the concept of charity as betterment acquired a new reality: from being an uplifting idea it became an urgent necessity that the poor should cease to be cogs in the industrial machine and learn instead to behave like proper human beings.

This concept had originated in the sympathy of the sixties towards the idea of the fundamental equality of mankind of which the Reform Act of 1867 was a symbol. With F. D. Maurice and Charles Kingsley as its prophets, this had found expression in charitable work in what was known as the betterment of the poor. The interest taken in the meetings in Liverpool of the National Association for the Promotion of Social Science in 1876 is significant of the attention which the idea now attracted. The emphasis placed at the Congress on the social education of the working man is in striking contrast to that on the improvement of his material conditions which had characterised the previous Liverpool meeting in 1858. The work of the Liverpool Council of Education, founded in 1874 with the aim of persuading the people to take advantage of the educational facilities now provided for their children, and the opening in the previous year of the first cocoa room of the British Workman's Public-house Company, were the subjects of papers.[15] The Meeting for Working Men held in St. George's Hall discussed art and science, and the Marquis of Huntly in his Presidential Address stated that wage increases of the working man should be accompanied by an increase " in the culture of his mind and the interests of his offspring ".[16]

The idea that the function of charity was to " better " the behaviour of the poorest classes was ultimately to become of the greatest importance. For the time being, lack of opportunity severely restricted its practical application. Almost the only society specifically organised for betterment was the Kyrle Society, founded in 1877 by leading local philanthropists. Named after John Kyrle, the Man of Ross, who had been noted for his efforts to provide amenities in his native town, the Liverpool society was one of several about the country, its aim being to bring pleasure into dull lives by such means as the beautifying of schools with decorative panelling,

[15] *Proceedings*, pp. 450, 382.
[16] *Ibid.*, pp. xxx, 3.

arranging for flowers to be sent from the country to town children, and organising Happy Evenings at Board Schools.[17] Of its somewhat dilettante activities the *Liverpool Daily Post* wrote that for the rich to share even the pleasure in flowers with the poor was " to make a tacit acknowledgement of the fact that all human lives are fundamentally alike, (which) would go further to reform the relations between them, than much of the charity which poverty is apt to regard as extorted from the scruples or the fears of wealth."[18]

The concern over the degeneration of the poor was thus largely frustrated, although to it must be credited the support given to such institutions as that of Mrs. Birt's Sheltering Homes which were devoted to the rescue of the most neglected and poorest.[19] Mrs. Birt came to Liverpool in 1873 on the invitation of the committee of the proposed home for children in course of emigration, work in connection with which her sister, Annie Macpherson, was already well-known in London and Liverpool. Mrs. Birt's approach was very different from that of the upper class women habitually associated with charity. She permitted herself a warmth of appeal which they had been trained to conceal: ladies flocked to attend her meetings, and it was said that the Town Hall was always damp after she had spoken. Deeply religious, she found her immediate inspiration in actual contact with the poorest of the poor. " To keep the heart soft and tender for these stray lambs, I occasionally take a day for visiting. Dear friends, I dare not describe to you the helpless misery, moral ruin, the filthy wretchedness I found these children in. . . . But that day's visiting brought a day of bed for me; I was sick in mind, body and spirit, overwhelmed by the awfulness of the lives which little children see and lead ".[20]

Mrs. Birt's emphasis on the need for warm and motherly love in work for poor children, the emotional quality of her appeals for support, and the lack of a merit test, were all in direct contradiction to the principles laid down by organised charity, though the scale and efficiency of her work were a tribute to the influence of the idea of method versus muddle in charitable work.

This was not, however, by any means the whole story. The emphasis on material success had endowed it with a positively religious sanctity, so that prosperity became the hallmark of virtue. From this it followed that, just as the individual was held to have failed in his moral duty if his industry was not crowned with success, so society was now felt to have failed since, however virtuous its intention, the existence of so numerous and permanent a class of wretched poor was obvious proof of its failure to reach a state of

[17] Ivy Ireland. *Margaret Beavan of Liverpool.* (Young, 1938.) p. 26.
[18] *Liverpool Daily Post*, 1st April, 1886.
[19] Lilian M. Birt. *The Children's Home-Finder.* (Nisbet, 1913.)
[20] *Ibid.*, p. 117.

grace. The rich as a class stood convicted, and individuals in it became aware of a sense of guilt towards God and, more immediately, man in the shape of the poor. This sense of guilt endowed personal service to the poor with an intrinsic merit because it was felt that it provided a means of expiation.

Purely conventional giving, and the philanthropy of the social climber, yielded in many to an inner compulsion to " do something " which, as will be seen later, often proved a hard taskmaster. The more acute the sense of guilt, the more numerous, degraded and desperate must be those to be served, till workers came to vie with each other in seeking out hitherto unknown degrees of horror and difficulty in their work, to the consternation of organised charity. Thus Samuel Smith, M.P., took over the abandoned Coliseum Theatre in Paradise Street, and after an abortive attempt to organize innocent amusements there, used it for Sunday evening services for the degraded. He said frankly that : " success was attained by giving a roll or small loaf of bread to each person who attended. This may be called a species of bribery, but we argued that a piece of dry bread could only be acceptable to a hungry man, and our object was to get at the lowest stratum of the population. We succeeded to our heart's content, for we had the place crammed each Sunday; and so many children came in with their parents, especially squalling babies in their mothers' arms, that the noise was like that of Pandemonium. At last we were obliged to separate the children and form a special meeting for them. . . . The filth and stench of the audience were indescribable. One could hardly walk through to the platform without feeling sick."[21] Incidentally, the Sunday School, which numbered about 1,000, was staffed by " some sixty teachers, many of them hard workers in shops all week ".

This sense of individual guilt was a new element in the relationship between rich and poor. True, Johns had long ago recognised his own share in the general responsibility for the condition of the people, whilst Thom's greatest attribute[22] had been a capacity for rousing in his hearers a sense of unsuspected obligations. Thom did on occasion use the word guilt in regard to the relationship with the poor, but only in reference to the failure of the rich to perform the obligations inherent in the possession of wealth. To the established upper classes, their relationship with the poor implied the acceptance of a great responsibility by a minority whose leadership was respected by and necessary to the dependent masses. This was explicit in William Rathbone's *Social Duties,* but it was by no means a point of view individual to him, as the paper read by A. B. Forwood to the Liverpool Diocesan Conference indicates:—" The relative positions in life thus occupied by the majority and minority of the people

[21] Samuel Smith, *op. cit.,* p. 106.
[22] See p. 34.

of this the second city in the Empire affords much food for reflection. It is an obligation incumbent upon the small minority in the land whom circumstances have placed in a position of comparative affluence and influence, to use these powers to afford to those in a less favoured position a chance to improve themselves. If the majority see that the minority of their fellow-countrymen thus use their riches and their position, they will lose that bitterness which neglect and callousness engender, class distinctions will be forgotten, and the great democracy will acquiesce in that healthful influence, which those with education, leisure, and means now happily exercise on the legislation of the country."[23] Their charity thus lacked the compulsion of guilt except in so far as they had failed to execute the obligations of their wealth; they were therefore able to withstand the emotional appeal of the wretchedness of the "undeserving" by reason of their conviction that to yield to their own pity would be to sin against the soul of the poor man.

The difference between this concept of charity and that of the newly roused middle classes was thus profound. There was, however, one bond which was common to them all, namely, a yearning to do good to the poor in person. Betterment, whether of the deserving or the undeserving, was best achieved by personal contact with those possessing a better way of life: guilt, whatever its source, sought relief in contact with the injured. This need to give personal service received additional strength from the fact that prosperity was proving unexpectedly insufficient to the Victorian, especially, as has been pointed out, to women. Life in a town of mutually exclusive suburbs, each based largely on a single social class, failed to provide the sense of security which comes from belonging to a balanced community. In other industrial towns, there was a certain homogenity of life centring on the mill or factory, but this the mercantile character of Liverpool's industry denied her. Men came to Liverpool to get, not to give. Social ambition dominated their behaviour, introducing formality and materialism at the expense of the human need to belong to and to serve a community. The result was a spiritual and emotional poverty which ill accorded with the material abundance of the times, and a dearth of opportunity for the practical expression of feelings of good will.

An admirable illustration of this point is provided by Sir Donald Currie's account of his early ventures into practical philanthropy. The group of young men whom he describes were obviously motivated as much by their own need to give as by any specific lack on the part of the poor. They yearned to do good, and to spread abroad the way of life they themselves thought desirable; and for these good intentions, the poor constituted a handy object.

. . . . "We sat down, twenty of us, and said we were all enjoy-

[23] A. B. Forwood. *Dwellings of the Industrial Classes.* 1883.

ing so much the association with each other that we must do something for others, and they asked me to deliver the essay. We every
week gave a subject upon which a young man was to write, and he
had to write it whether he knew anything about it or not. My text
was 'Let us provoke one another to good works', and so, two by
two we were sent apostolic like—we were sent on our own authority—down to the docks, and the first Sunday night we had 400 wild
young savage children to deal with. Lights were put out, forms
upset, teachers rubbed against and laughed at. But they became subsequently so docile that you could lift a finger and they would say
no more. Boys were got into ships and as clerks into offices.
Children who were sick were visited at night. There was brought out
of that dense population the most encouraging Christian results. . . .
I will say a word or two on the beneficial effects on the young men
themselves."[24]

The urgency of this need to forge a close connection with the
community by means of service is a by-product of the industrial
society whose significance has not been fully appreciated. Its effect
upon charitable effort was eventually to transform the very nature
of benevolence, replacing the almsgiving philanthropist of tradition
by the voluntary worker of the twentieth century.

Nevertheless, to talk thus of the inspiration to charitable work in
terms of personal need to give service, and of a guilty conscience,
must not for one moment be allowed to obscure the fact that the
new light which their own anxiety cast upon the scene revealed to
the middle classes the desperate plight of vast numbers of their
fellow-men to which they had previously been blind, and roused in
many of them a deep sense of pity which was akin to love.

It was one thing to yearn to serve the poor, however, but quite
another to decide upon precise ways and means of doing so. The
inadequacy of the existing benevolent societies, and the obvious ill-
effect of indiscriminate giving, had brought charitable effort into
such question, if not actual disrepute, that Farrie wrote in *Toiling
Liverpool*:

"I doubt whether charity is doing any good at all to society. . . .
If you are going to do nothing else, if you are going to satisfy your
conscience on the one hand, and provide a doubtful safety valve
against social upheaval on the other, by lavish charity, then I say
without the slightest hesitation that it would be better to let the
destitute—men, women, and children—die of cold and hunger in
the streets". A storm of argument broke out over Farrie's conclusion that charity in such circumstances was more likely to do harm
than good. Most people thought that to help the starving poor was

[24] Sir Donald Currie at the Jubilee Reunion of the Young Men's Society.
Quoted in *Canning Street Presbyterian Church*, 1846-96, (Read and Co.,
1896), p. 55.

H

a right and proper thing to do, and to argue that out of such good evil might result was dubbed too subtle and too unpractical to be worthy of consideration.

In any case, betterment being as yet only an idea, there seemed to be no alternative way of dealing with the poorest of the poor. Poor Law reform was regarded as dull and uninteresting: social improvement by means of municipal government was not attractive to gentlemen, and certainly not suitable for ladies. As for state "interference", it is a measure of the extent to which the public were already jolted out of the rut of the past forty years that the idea of collective action should so rapidly have come to be considered as at least a subject for discussion. Mr. A. B. Forwood went so far as to say that "Liverpool is a very remarkable illustration—if any justification is needed—of the necessity of public control, to ensure health and to save the toiling thousands from the evil consequences which the avarice and greed of individuals might inflict". Liverpool was in fact setting a remarkable example of municipal activity in what had previously been regarded a strictly individual sphere of action, and although this was inspired by necessity rather than principle, it was to provide a sound foundation upon which the social services of future years were to be built. Meanwhile, so far as charity was concerned, such a solution failed to satisfy the longing to serve the poor in person which now motivated increasing numbers. Indeed, the main argument put forward against state intervention in matters of common welfare was that, judging from past experience, it was impossible for the state to be personal: the Central Relief Society met with strong opposition because, like the Poor Law, its relief was administered by officials on the instructions of a committee whose contact with their clients was reduced to a minimum.

The Central Relief Society had originally been formed in precisely similar circumstances, and subsequent events had seemed to justify the principles then evolved of giving relief only after careful consideration and inquiry into each individual case. The question now raised, however, was the much more serious one of whether, even if these principles could be extended to cover the whole field of charitable relief, the answer to the problem of poverty really lay with philanthropy. The thought that charity in the accepted sense of almsgiving, however desirable a virtue in the rich, might be irrelevant to the present needs of the poor was a disturbing one. The Central Relief Society fixed as its principles were, found itself faced with a difficult situation. It had already been forced by pressure of circumstances to move a considerable distance from its original object of the methodical and organised relief of the deserving. Thus the ultimate lesson of the fire lighter scheme[25]

25 Farrie. *op. cit.*

was the unpalatable conclusion that there was in the town a surplus of casual labour greater than even the fluctuating demands of trade required which raised the awkward question of whether it was the function of charity to deal with this problem. If work was not found for the unemployed amongst their applicants, of what use was temporary relief, however discriminate? The Society compromised by helping men to improve their employability, and to find work in other districts, but the actual provision of work they regarded as being beyond the province of charity. The work of charity, they had always maintained, and now re-affirmed, was to rescue the chance sufferer from ill-luck or ill-health, and to administer relief on principles which would restore the recipient to a state of moral grace and industry. For all those who fell outside this definition, the Poor Law, and the many forms of spiritual agency must be responsible. Awkward though these problems as to the proper object of their charity might be, on the actual administration of relief no doubts were entertained. The methods of discriminate giving, which paid greater heed to the ultimate self-respect of the recipient than to his immediate need, had been proved over and over again to be the only workable alternative to the intimate acquaintance upon which the old charity of neighbour-to-neighbour had been based. Nevertheless, though they had found a contemporary equivalent in charitable method, the Society was well aware that its use of officials in the administration of relief lacked the warmth and the uplifting influence which could only be derived from personal contact between rich and poor. Previously, the spur to reform had been lacking. Now, faced by a problem whose magnitude might seem to put it beyond hope of voluntary remedy, they set themselves the fantastically difficult task of so organising their benevolence as to secure the efficiencies of collective action on the basis of the individual and voluntary act of charity.[26]

William Rathbone in his book on *Social Duties* in 1867 had visualized a central charitable agency which would organise voluntary workers, record their experiences, and stimulate and guide subscribers. A year or two later, he had followed this up by a visit to Elberfeld in Germany, where a similar scheme was in operation, with the important difference that there the whole of the work of relieving the poor was undertaken by voluntary workers. At this point, his Parliamentary work had intervened, but in 1886, seeking for an outlet for the feelings roused by the death of his son in a boating accident, Mr. Rathbone turned his attention to the possibility of putting into practice his original scheme. He persuaded the Local Government Board to send an inspector to Elberfeld, and arranged for him to be accompanied by the Society's chief agent, Mr. Hanewinkel, and by Mr. Loch of the

[26] Domestic Mission Report, 1879-80.

London Charity Organisation Society, hoping that their reports would enable the Society to come to some decision. The Reports of the two experimental committees which had meanwhile been set up in Liverpool were indecisive,[27] but the bad winter of 1887 imposed such a severe strain upon the machinery of the Society that some reorganisation was inevitable. Meanwhile public opinion on the whole problem of poverty had been roused, and the supporters of organised charity had been compelled to admit that the system of discrimination had resulted in a loss of those personal contacts which were now recognised to be of such importance.

"The conclusion to be drawn is that one effective means of raising the poor is the mixing with them, on a thoroughly friendly footing, of those whose position and character are higher than their own. In London, the experiment is being tried of getting University men to go down amongst the poor in this way. But why should this be confined to the University men? For my own part, I should like to see a band of earnest Christian workers—women as well as men—with hearts and heads in the right place, going in and out amongst the poor, not merely as religious visitors, but (while not neglecting this) sharing their joys and sorrows, lightening their burdens, bringing their wider knowledge to help them to meet the trials of life, firmly, though lovingly, correcting their errors and graver faults—

'With a patient hand removing
All the briars from the way',

and when adversity comes, directing them where suitable help may be had. . . ."[28]

The original experiment was therefore expanded gradually to cover the whole town, over each district of which presided a committee of Friendly Visitors. The preliminary enquiries into each case were made by paid officials, but its subsequent handling was the responsibility of the Visitor in whose particular section it fell, and whose accounts and decisions were submitted to the District Committee. Who these visitors actually were it is hard to discover, though many of the names are familiar; and the backbone of the committees would seem to have been provided by people personally inspired by Mr. Rathbone's own enthusiasm for the idea. The ordinary middle classes took slowly to the work, whilst his suggestion that working-class people should be utilised seems never to have been pursued.[29]

If he had not been so deeply involved in politics Mr. Rathbone might have repeated with this scheme his success with the District

[27] Annual Report, 1886 and 1887.

[28] W. Grisewood, *op. cit.*

[29] Annual Report, 1886. It is amusing to note that the topical equivalent of looking like a social worker was to look like a District Visitor.

Nursing Society. As it was, though there were eventually 23 District Committees with some three hundred or more visitors,[30] right from the start their reports sound a note of discouragement. Their almost complete failure in any direction except the administration of relief,[31] the capricious intervention of weather and fluctuations of trade, the indifference of the poor themselves towards their own betterment, depressed the voluntary workers, and filled them with a sense of futility. The relationship between the ladies and gentlemen of the committees and the men and women who sought their aid remained one of patronage rather than friendship. The very zeal of their attack upon the evils of indiscriminate giving turned the intention of friendly intimacy into a probing and prying which provoked in the poor irritation and dislike instead of gratitude and affection. Above all, the strict definition of charity as extending only to the deserving failed to satisfy the deep concern of the charitable for the degenerate and degraded.

To the middle classes the issue was not clear but they were certain that to rule out the unworthy, the intemperate and lazy and degenerate, was to rule out the very people whose condition stirred them to compunction. These, and not the virtuous poor, were the people who had spurned the accepted morality of the commercial community; these were the people who must be re-infected with the conviction of the desirability of security and responsibility; these were the people they longed to help. Accordingly they turned away from organised charity, although they could as yet see no alternative.

That these very people might themselves contribute to their own salvation was an idea which was not yet to be entertained, and of what the poor thought, little was heard. The new life in the Trade Union movement undoubtedly attracted the more lively amongst them; in others the ingrained habit of relying upon the interest of the prosperous, discouraged the expression of any sentiment but that of at least superficial gratitude. One instance alone remains of working-class charity in the strict sense of the word, though the annals of the friendly societies might reveal others. This was a Dock Labourers' Relief Fund, which was founded in 1885 with a capital of £5, and was sponsored by a Mr. Scott, who presumably raised further money as required. Being the only one of its kind, it deserves quotation:

" On a little low form sit two elderly members of the committee— grey, silent, heavy-looking men, who have the curious appearance of inward communion, which the intelligent elderly labourer so often acquires. These two committee men sit during the whole evening,

[30] Mr. Rathbone had visualized the necessity for some 2,500 visitors, each giving two hours a week, but he seems never to have been fully convinced of the practicability of this.

[31] e.g., Annual Report for 1888.

never exchanging a word, keenly scrutinising each applicant who comes in, and the impostor would indeed be clever who could deceive their long experience and intimate knowledge of their labouring brethren. . . . On one desk lies a great string of tallies, each of which represents 2/- in food, payable by a neighbouring provision dealer. A big committee man stands at the door, admits the applicants, and demands their names. Another burly fellow, wearing the silver cross of the Temperance League of the Holy Cross, a beaming, bustling, genial man, stands in the middle of the room with the tallies, conducting an acute cross-examination of the applicants. If he does not know his man, he probes and tests him with an ingenuity worthy of an Old Bailey lawyer. These men, who work the charity themselves, for their fellows, we may even say for their fellow-sufferers, for they are poor enough themselves, have no intention of being imposed upon, and their work is done with a business-like order and unfailing intelligence which many a more ambitious charity might with advantage imitate. The big man with the silver cross is familiarly addressed by Mr. Scott as " Barney ". Barney pegs away with his cross-examination until Mr. Scott, whose compassion is easily touched, interrupts with " Oh, give him an order, Barney! ", and Barney, nothing loth, hands the coveted talisman to the shivering fellow, singing out at the same time to the silent record-keeper in the corner, " An order, Mr. Murphy ". And this goes on for hours and hours, until frequently midnight is reached."[32]

It would, however, be unfair to leave the matter there. There can be no doubt that to search for leaders amongst the spiritless mass of the people must have seemed like searching for needles in haystacks, and there was the further difficulty that those who had any ambition to improve their status, moved off to better districts whenever they could. The churches were, in fact, sometimes criticised because the effect of their work was to inspire the removal from bad neighbourhoods of the very elements of decency whose influence was so urgently required.

In any case, the encouragement of schemes for practical self-help amongst the working-class bore little relation to the middle class longing to do good to others, the proper satisfaction of which was as important a function of charitable effort as concern for the needs of the poor. The last decade of the century was to demonstrate the validity of this point when for lack of guidance, the immense asset of the middle-class enthusiasm for charity was extravagantly spent on what became known as slumming.

[32] Farrie. *Op. cit.*

CHAPTER VIII

CHARITY FRUSTRATED: " SLUMMING ". 1885-1900.

THE continuing state of economic uncertainty which had set in with the eighteen-eighties, and the painful awakening to the true condition of the people which had accompanied it, together with the lack of any obvious solution, gave rise to a mood of despair and depression. " Another year's work completed and God only knows how much of it has been worthily done ", groaned one of the Domestic Missioners.[1] " All we can do is painfully to feel and wearily to iterate that something is wrong ", was *Porcupine's* version.[2] Well might Liverpool despond, for conditions there were still worse than almost anywhere else in the kingdom, and their remedy correspondingly hard to find. The state of the poor defied analysis, the material poverty of their lives matched only by their spiritual necessities, their physical ill-health by their moral degeneration. Their utter indifference to their own good, even to life itself, found vent in a thriftlessness, intemperance and brutality,[3] which at once appalled and repelled the prosperous, deepening the gulf between the two.

It was, indeed, more difficult to see whence inspiration or help were to come than to determine the nature of the problems to be solved. Disillusionment as to the relevance of either charity or religion to such problems had gained ground; it was obvious that no one would ever be led to mend his ways by Act of Parliament, and the scientific treatment of social problems seemed a day-dream. The Earl of Derby spoke for the whole community when as Lord Mayor he said that the poor would be always with them, and they must just deal with those questions as they arose, as best they could.[4] Charles Booth, although by this time he had moved from Liverpool to London, expressed the common reaction when he said that : — " It is the sense of helplessness that tries everyone. . . . The wage-earners are helpless to regulate or obtain the value of their work; the manufacturer or dealer can only work within the limits of competition; the rich are helpless to relieve want without stimulating its sources; the legislature is helpless because the limits of successful interference by change of law are circumscribed closely."[5]

[1] Domestic Mission Annual Report, 1887.
[2] *Porcupine*, 5th October, 1889.
[3] The Liverpool Society for the Prevention of Cruelty to Children was founded in 1883, the first of its kind in this country.
[4] C.R.S. Annual Report, 1895.
[5] Quoted in Webb, *op. cit.*, p. 270.

In this mood, public opinion was ready to welcome any positive statement, and the dramatic juxtaposition of William Booth's *In Darkest England*[6] with Stanley's *In Darkest Africa* in 1890 attracted immediate attention. Booth's book crystallised the feelings which had been accumulating during recent years, and its influence as a stimulus to action was felt throughout the entire field of social work. The interest aroused by the book in Liverpool was remarkable. The local campaigns against prostitution and the drink trade, for instance, made quite startling progress after years of mere plodding. General Booth was received by neighbouring Mayors. He spoke at a meeting in Hengler's Circus, and his visit was followed by a lengthy and spirited newspaper correspondence. His book was discussed in leading articles, and no public meeting could take place without reference to it. No bazaar was opened, no study circle held, without the General's plan receiving mention. Even the Civic Service reflected the new vitality: "It is no exaggeration to say that the sermon preached to the Mayor and Corporation at St. Peter's on Sunday, was a startling surprise for the kid-gloved and well-dressed congregation. Instead of the usual conventional homily, Canon Cross thundered on the moral evils of our city, and in high flights of thrilling eloquence reminded the City Fathers of their responsibilities and duties. His description of the 'atmosphere reeking with the drunkard's profanity and the air phosphorescent with the ghastly reel of the painted prostitute' visibly impressed his hearers".[7]

In vain the established societies protested that they had been in existence for years to do precisely what the General hoped to do: nobody was interested in the old familiar story of prostitution, drink and bad housing which they had to tell. The vigorous emotional tone of the General, the brisk determination with which he proposed to strike at the very existence of poverty,[8] and his conviction that the poor as a class could be regenerated into industrious and respectable beings, made an instant appeal to the middle classes, and such support as he secured on Merseyside came chiefly from them. However, his idea of social planning was too foreign to the traditional conception of charity to be of interest to the existing societies, who consequently failed to reap the benefit of the enthusiasm roused by the General. The general public was thus left to find its own means of expressing its new impulse to charity.

This was not far to seek. Just as the working classes had earlier become merged with the poor, so the poor now became synonymous with the unemployed, constituting a social problem which challenged

[6] General Booth. *In Darkest England.* (Salvation Army, 1890.)

[7] *Porcupine,* 22nd November, 1890.

[8] His plan was designed to organise training and employment so that every man should have a fair opportunity of earning his own living or of migrating to more promising fields.

every accepted tenet of the individualist philosophy. The general public were quick to respond. To them it was plain that talk disparaging to indiscriminate charity might " suit some drawing-rooms, but when a person of feeling, and with help at command, came in contact with a starving mother with four or five children in a similar condition, such considerations of the brain melted away, and the heart dictated the course of action despite the fact of the husband being drunken or reprobate ".[9]

Shocked by the orgy of charity which ensued, the Central Relief Society struggled to combine its long-term principles with schemes for immediate and wholesale relief. Its endeavours met with considerable hostility. The poor themselves had little doubt that discriminate charity provided no answer to their problems. They resented having to submit to inquiry in order to obtain through charity what they were coming to think should be theirs by right[10]: they refused to express gratitude for what was their due. A deputation of unemployed men and women told the Lord Mayor in the desperate Spring of 1893, when to lack of work was added exceptionally hard weather, that they had resolved to have nothing to do with the Central Relief Society, adding that " the Relief Society's work in Park Lane was only a sweating wood-chopping manufactory. It was not charity. It was a place where men worked, and were not well paid for what they did. The saws they had to work with were like hoop iron ".[11]   The *Liverpool Daily Post* suggested that investigation of the Society's affairs by a small committee of inquiry would relieve it of such accusations. To which the Society replied in a discreet note in the following Annual Report that though much of the work could not be estimated in terms of relief paid out, yet the fact that nearly four thousand pounds had been spent on relief, including Soup Kitchens and the Workshops at a cost of £880 in administration, proved the efficiency of their methods.

Within ten of the worst weeks of the Spring of 1893, five thousand families were relieved by the Central Relief Society, and after the crisis was over, a careful report on the whole situation was presented to the Unemployed Commission set up by the Lord Mayor, on which three women served, one of whom was Miss Florence Melly. The findings of this Commission were a victory for organised charity: " one of the most powerful contributory factors in this problem is the practice of injudicious and indiscriminate charity. It ought to be regarded as a grave social offence to give

[9] Special Appeal Meeting of the League of Welldoers. 3rd Annual Report, 1895.

[10] *e.g.*, Domestic Mission, Annual Report, 1888.

[11] *Liverpool Daily Post*, 20th February, 1893.

[12] C.R.S. Annual Report, 1895.

money, or goods convertible into money, to any casual applicant with whose circumstances the donor is not acquainted ".[13]

The Commission reported in favour of administering relief through Voluntary District Visitors thus giving a timely spur to the enlistment of workers by the Central Relief Society. The provision of work by voluntary societies, Poor Law Guardians, or indeed any other body, they regarded as dangerous because it might be taken to imply the right of a man to work, and the duty of the state to provide facilities for him to do so. The importance of organising constant employment for their men was, however, tactfully urged upon the employers.

In February, 1895, an even more desperate situation developed, when to the decrease of work caused by the Lancashire cotton strike and the decline in the volume of shipping was added another winter of outstanding severity. The Central Relief Society with the experience of previous crises behind it, hastily opened up its Soup Kitchens, issued Relief Tickets to the Police for distribution at their discretion, and opened free shelters in Mission Halls. The Board of Guardians gave extra relief and the Lord Mayor opened a Special Relief Fund to aid established societies, to whom the Central Relief Society also distributed Relief Tickets. " It was hoped that these measures would have been deemed sufficient to meet all cases of actual need. The public, however, were led to believe that there were large numbers of people in danger of immediate starvation, and began to give relief broadcast; tradesmen distributing bread and other relief at their shops, Churches and Chapels opening Soup Kitchens, and funds being raised for immediate distribution in all directions. Many thousands of soup, bread and cocoa tickets were purchased by the public from this Society, and frequently given away at once, indiscriminately, in the streets.

" The result was as might be expected that the relief thus given, entirely without discrimination, and without any concert between these various classes, produced great demoralisation, much of it going into the same hands, and these, in many instances, persons who were not at all in need of charity. Of 33,500 of the Society's soup tickets issued through the Police, only 24,716 had been presented up to three weeks afterwards, and of 24,000 sold to the public, and which, as stated above, were mostly sold for immediate distribution, only 15,626 had been presented. Numerous instances have come under notice in which both grown-up persons and children have been found in possession of a considerable number of relief tickets issued by different agencies. In one case six penny bread tickets are said to have been sold for three pence. In several instances the Committee have learned of people being supplied with

[13] *Commission of Inquiry into the Subject of the Unemployed in the City of Liverpool,* reporting in 1894.

three to five different cwts. of coal on charity tickets in one week, and in one case a coal dealer delivered a cwt. of coal to a person who already had about half-a-ton of coal in his yard. People presenting orders for bread and groceries asked for entirely different things from those named on the tickets, in some cases wanting money and in others what might properly be termed luxuries, a clear evidence that they were not urgently in need of the necessaries of life. Boys presented charity tickets and asked for tinned salmon, Eccles cakes and cheese cakes. Women sought relief whose husbands were at work; children ran about the streets in order to get the tickets so lavishly given away, often without the knowledge or consent of their parents and information has been received on good authority that in some districts it was impossible to secure the attendance of the children at the schools on this account. Basket girls and hawkers ceased to ply their trades and took to begging. A further evil is that persons have been drawn into the town from other places, and are likely, if they remain, to swell the number of the Unemployed, and to increase the difficulty of obtaining employment in the future. Another result has been that many Bakers, Grocers and Eating and Lodging House-keepers have suffered considerable loss through their usual customers going elsewhere with charity tickets.

" It was stated at Meetings of the Board of Guardians that the Vagrant Sheds of the Workhouses were deserted, their usual occupants availing themselves of the Shelters provided for the homeless ".[14]

Yet though reason might agree that all this and more could indeed be laid at the door of indiscriminate charity, emotion backed up by guilty conscience found it impossible to refuse the appeal of the gloomy, gaunt and dismal crowds, and once more the public rushed to their relief. The *Daily Post* again wrote stinging leaders on the parsimony of the Central Relief Society which with all its vast income was yet so grudging in its alms giving, and accusing it of spending on inquiry and administration the alms which had been entrusted to it for distribution.[15]

With the improvement of weather and trade, the immediate crisis passed. No solution had been found for the problem of unemployment, but this much progress had at least been made, that casual labour with its periodic decline into outright unemployment, had emerged as a specific problem quite definitely outside the scope of charity. The effect on charitable effort was striking. It was as if the public had sensed the absurdity of trying to cope on the basis of individual charity with the mass of misery caused by unemploy-

[14] Central Relief Society. *Memorandum on the Late Distress*, February, 1895.

[15] *e.g., Liverpool Daily Post*, 12th February, 1895.

ment; without waiting for legislation to catch up with them, they shifted their interest and support to more promising pursuits.[16]

The truth was that the campaign on behalf of discriminate charity had been all too convincing. The scenes accompanying the distribution of free food on St. George's Plateau, the tales of duplicity and deceit, the theorising of economists and moralists, had all served to sow doubt in the minds of the potentially charitable. The effect, however, was not to convert them to more methodical giving, but simply to divert their thoughts to other ways of " doing good ". Released from the perplexities which had attended their attempts to help the unemployed, they looked about them for alternatives, and quickly became aware of the possibilities of the existing movement for the betterment of the poor. This fitted their needs exactly. The ideal of betterment was in complete contrast to the relief-giving associated with the unemployed or with organised charity, and was, moreover, aimed at removing precisely those attributes of poverty which most disturbed the middle classes. In addition, since betterment could best be achieved by personal contact, such work made an instant appeal to their own yearning to give service.

Here stood clearly revealed for the first time in years, a task which the charitable public felt to be within its competence. The confusions of economic theory, the red herrings of philosophy, sank into insignificance before a rising conviction that in the reformation of the poor lay the solution to their present unhappy condition, and that this was a duty which only voluntary charity could perform. The vague conception of betterment crystallised out in terms of personal service: the emphasis in charitable work shifted from the material offerings of the benevolent to the intrinsic merits of the service they were so anxious to render, from the tangible benefits of coals and tea to the intangibles of friendship and culture.

The idea of setting about the social problem by means of personally improving the behaviour of the poor offered fresh hope to a public jaded by its failure to get to grips with the material misery of the unemployed. Hardly a charity but reflects its influence. Appeals for financial support stressed the character-strengthening aspects of the work of the various charities: it was on their value in developing habits of obedience and teaching the benefit of submitting to rule and restraint that Father Nugent, and his successor, Father Berry, based appeal for support for the boys' homes with which their names are associated.[17] Clubs for young people, so far

---

[16] Not, of course, that the distress of the unemployed ceased to concern the philanthropic, or that individuals ceased to experiment with schemes for the cure of unemployment, but that the responsibility for relief ceased to overshadow every other form of charity.

[17] The Very Rev. Canon Bennett. *Father Nugent of Liverpool*. (Liverpool Catholic Children's Protection Society, 1949).

merely preventive now acquired a new importance as a means of character training. But the fact that all of these depended for their success on the personal service of the charitable constituted their greatest attraction for the public, and the voluntary worker became as characteristic a feature of the closing years of the century as the voluntary society had been of its opening. The bulk of these newcomers to charitable work were drawn from the middle classes. Such people lacked the cultural background, and even more important, the foundation of spiritual faith which would have made it possible for them to approach social problems with anything like detachment. What they lacked in intellectual training or spiritual discipline, they more than made up for in intensity of feeling. To refuse the loving word and generous gesture for the calm calculation of cause and effect was to them a crime: they felt present suffering to be of greater moment than future damnation. H. Lee J. Jones stands out amongst this largely anonymous band of volunteers, because he is at once typical of them all, and was himself a pioneer in the introduction of the middle classes into social work. That a man should emerge as representative of a group so largely comprised of women is only an apparent paradox; women had not yet become vocal on the subject of charity, nor were they offered any opportunity to make an individual name for themselves.

Very little is known about Lee Jones' early life. He was born at Runcorn in 1870, and educated at Liverpool College, which implies parents of at least moderate means. It is said that he was intended to take orders in the Church of England. Early in his twenties, inspired by a casual visit to the slums, he interviewed those who, as school managers or clergymen, were concerned about the low diet on which many children in the poorer parts of the city were being brought up. Finding that a number were anxious to start some sort of school meals scheme, but were defeated by the overhead costs involved, he quickly formed a large committee, including twenty-two assorted clergymen but no women, of whose services, however, he seldom seems to have availed himself. Although he was unknown, funds were in some remarkable fashion forthcoming, and in 1893 the Liverpool Food Association was founded under the presidency of the City Coroner, with Lee Jones as Honorary Secretary. Premises in Limekiln Lane in the Scotland Road district were secured, and soup boilers erected. Eleven schools were catered for in the first season, the meals being sent to them in special containers by horse-drawn float, and distributed by the teachers: spoons of britannia metal and enamelled plates were provided and each child was given " four-fifths of a pint of savoury and nutritious soup, compounded on chemical calculation, and a slice of currant roll or bread and jam as he or she passes out of school."[18] The dinners

[18] Annual Report, 1893.

were sold at ½d. each, the teachers determining which pupils might
be described as ".richly deserving" of the privilege of cheap meals.
It had been anticipated that the scheme would become self-supporting, but it was soon realised that this was impracticable since there
were so many children whose needs were evident but whose
ha'pennies were not, to whom free meals had to be given.

The school meals scheme was followed by one for the service
of food to invalids in their own homes by voluntary Lady
Attendants. The change of title in 1898 to the more comprehensive
Liverpool Food and Betterment Association was significant of the
enlarging scope of its activity and, of course, of the general trend of
social work. Each succeeding scheme opened up new vistas of need
and the relieving of one distress merely revealed the urgency of a
dozen more. One of the best known of these early ventures was that
of open-air concerts to be given in courts and alleys " to elevate the
seared mind or brighten the dulled hour amongst the poor and the
poorest poor ". But to describe single activities is to touch only a
fraction of Lee Jones' work. He progressed from Articles to Aid
and Please Invalids to Sandwichmen's Dinners,[19] from Ragpickers'
Suppers to Beds for the Homeless, through Midnight Meals, First
Aid, and Annual Re-clothes to the National Fund for the Prevention
of Suicide through Poverty. The poorest poor were in every case
given preference, and their problems were tackled by every method
from journalism to temperance, from entertainment to catering.

The considerable labour obviously involved in all this was undertaken by men and women whose names are now mere ciphers: they
sometimes receive mention in the Association's Reports but who
or what they were it is impossible to discover. Lee Jones possessed
a flair for arousing an interest in his work in those " who did not
give, and who appeared as if they would not give, but who seemed
to be amassing their money for the purpose of taking it with them
to the grave ".[20] His lists of voluntary workers and of subscribers[21]
are impressive. Chance remarks suggest that the majority were
ordinary middle class people whom the charitable agencies had so
far tended to ignore. A music teacher is held up for emulation
because her pupils gave a concert in aid of funds. A chemist is
approved who, extracting teeth in his spare time, put the fees into
an Association collecting box. The death is recorded of the chief

---

[19] Consisting of Irish Stew with oysters and plum-pudding, all served " by
merry hearted ladies and gentlemen ". Annual Report of the Food and
Betterment Association, 1899.

[20] Annual Report of the Food and Betterment Association, 1899.

[21] The Association's subscription lists compare favourably with those of
older and more conventional organisations, running to three or four
thousand names. A certain number of leading citizens contributed the
conventional guinea or so, but the bulk of the subscribers were apparently
unknown and not well off, the amount they sent being often quite trivial.

clerk to the City Engineer, a loyal worker, whose wife had been a Lady Attendant before her marriage. It is significant that practically none of them appear in Liverpool's *Legion of Honour*.

His methods of finance were also original, a medley of effort which produced a maximum of result. An orgy of sentiment, the inspiration of all and sundry to the most ardent begging, the presentation of the cost of charity with the skill of an advertising agent, the absence of any accounts, the acceptance of funds from sources of which Lee Jones himself openly disapproved; in all this the only guiding principle was the urgency of the need of the poor, against which any accountancy of income or expenditure was simply irrelevant.

Yet busy and successful though he apparently was, his life was consumed by his sense of the compelling necessity for self-sacrifice in those who would serve the poor. He lived a spartan life from the age of twenty-four when he first went to Limekiln Lane, working without ceasing day after day, year in, year out, driving himself even more cruelly than he tried to drive others. State action within the sphere of charity he simply would not contemplate, and his League of Welldoers was a deliberate protest " against an increasing, professional, over-paid philanthropy ".[22] The League consisted of those who responded to his Call to a Higher Life by giving themselves up to the service of the Association in return for not more than £15 per annum, a uniform, and board and lodging of considerable austerity, their object being to sustain and ennoble, or alternatively, to relieve and refine, the poor. But though the name of the whole organisation was changed from the Food and Betterment Association to the League of Welldoers in 1909 it is apparent that Lee Jones had no idea what to do with it. There were conferences, and exhortations to raise money, but no clear-cut conception of any new relationship between suburb and slum emerges, and for lack of it, the League which might have been the climax of his work, failed to achieve reality. To live in poverty simply for poverty's sake did not help the genuine poor, whatever satisfactions it conveyed to those who did so.

The story of Lee Jones' life makes bitter reading. It reveals a man in search of something vital to his own happiness, turning to new venture after new venture in the hope that there would lie redemption, falling back perpetually unsatisfied and disappointed. And all to no apparent satisfaction. As early as 1897, he cried unhappily "I have ungrudgingly denied myself wordly prospects, made my permanent abode amongst the poorest poor, and toiled an average of fourteen hours a day, generally seven days per week, for five years. Must my little gold go too? Up to the present, it works

[22] Annual Report of the Food and Betterment Association, 1903.

out that I have paid over £100 a year for the privilege ".[23] With this complaint that others left him to do all the work went an envy of the indifference of others which reveals him as being at the mercy of an over-active conscience, a state he shared with many of the social reformers to whose fanaticism the social services of this country owe so much.[24]

Lee Jones' experience was typical of that of many who were then entering upon social work for the first time. For all their sincerity, for all their self-sacrifice, the impression remains one of frustration. These were moles, digging their way through a mountain of poverty, united by no common purpose and sharing no common faith.[25] And for lack of purpose, the vague longing to " do good ", to be of service to the community and so to achieve the happy security of being indispensable, which surely lay behind the slumming movement, failed to achieve permanence, and from it emerged no established principle to guide the charitable efforts of future generations.

Yet Lee Jones' contribution, and that of the great regiment of self-inspired martyrs whom he represents, must not therefore be lightly written off. There can be no doubt that the poor derived something far beyond old clothes and free soup from their association with him and with the League of Welldoers. The final justification of the man was the sincere passion of the grief with which he was mourned by those whom he had served. With all his shortcomings, he gave to the poor the inestimable conviction of his need of them, which is but another name for love. In so doing he and others like him, stood for a reminder of the essentially human quality of the charitable relationship, of which the urban society of his day and organised charity in particular, stood in danger of forgetting.

To many the 'nineties were a time of frustration, of wasted effort and aimless self-sacrifice. Personal service, whether as a Welldoer or a Friendly Visitor, stood for no more than a refusal to accept as permanent the gulf between the mass of misery amongst the poor and the inadequacy of the provision for its relief. However valuable this stand might be, it constituted only a protest and not a solution. Despondently, some turned to politics as providing a more hopeful

---

[23] Annual Report of the Food and Betterment Association, 1897.

[24] To this same cause can perhaps be attributed that calculated disregard for personal appearances which became such an unfortunate characteristic of the social worker of the early twentieth century. Lee Jones' comment on a visit to the Newsboys' Home at Everton was to ask: " Why some of the workers' display of jewellery, silks, and a single, fop-like eye-glass? Tut, tut!   Do differently this year, I *humbly* pray you ".   *Social Beacon,* January, 1895.

[25] It is striking to note how seldom in all the torrent of commentary which accompanied Lee Jones' life any reference to an ideal occurs.

solution, and this was notably the case amongst women. Yet help was already at hand, and evidence of the arrival of the " new " in charitable effort was nowhere more obvious than amongst the very ranks of the Central Relief Society itself. In true Liverpool tradition, and despite the adverse comment of the times as to the vitality of the old families, leadership came once more from that liberal group which had so consistently set the standard in local affairs, though the daughters were now to outstrip the sons.

I

CHAPTER IX

THE NEW PHILANTHROPY: "THE SOCIAL WORKER". 1890-1909.

THE entry upon a new century symbolised most aptly the sense of beginning a new age, of change and transition, which dominated the preceding decade. " It was to be an age of democracy, of social justice, of faith in the possibilities of the common man ".[1] This was reflected in the approach to the problems of poverty which the 'nineties dubbed new, but which in fact owed its origin to the dawning respect for the individual of thirty years before. Its influence had been apparent in charitable work for some time, and the betterment movement, for example, was based on the belief that even the most degenerate of men was still a human being, and must be helped to realise himself as such.[2] Experience had made plain the futility of promoting the betterment of the individual whilst leaving untouched his social surroundings: it was useless to reform the drunkard when the only society available to him was that of the public-house. The development of clubs amongst boys and girls was evidence of the consequent interest in work with groups rather than individuals. Its obvious economy in man-power led Lee Jones to base his work almost entirely on the collection of the poor into groups according to their needs, although the Central Relief Society maintained that relief should only be given on a family basis.

Respect for the individual had however, a more profound influence on charitable work in that, carried to its logical conclusion, it involved not merely the betterment of individuals, but the virtual extermination of poverty itself. The conditions revealed by *Squalid Liverpool*, for example, simply could not be accepted as permanent. The contemporary interest in science caused renewed efforts to be made to apply scientific methods to the solution of social problems, which revealed the lack of exact knowledge regarding the state of the poor. This led Charles Booth to doubt the very existence of poverty and so to embark on his Survey of London which set the pattern for many subsequent inquiries.[3] At the same time, the attempt to analyse the problems of poverty emphasised the consciousness of their complexity which already depressed voluntary workers, and laid the foundations for the eventual demand for training in charitable work.

[1] R. C. K. Ensor. *England, 1870-1914.* (Oxford: Clarendon Press, 1936). p. 527.

[2] A local girls' club owed its origin to the belief that " even rope-walk girls " were human.

[3] Charles Booth was said to be living about 1892 " in a lodging in Liverpool at an address unknown to his friends, making preliminary observations for a full study of the poverty of Liverpool ". *English Social Movements.* Wood. (Swan Sonnerschein and Co., 1895), p. 216.

124

This "new" approach was obviously foreign to the habitual charity of the nineteenth century, and gained support only amongst the more progressive. Meanwhile, the middle classes had developed their enthusiasm for "slumming", and organised charity had concentrated on the mechanics of almsgiving to such an extent that they might well have ended in fatally overlying the new ideas in philanthropy had it not been for the close relationship which had developed between charitable work and the movement for the emancipation of women. The story of the new in charitable theory and practice can, in fact, be told largely in terms of the contribution made by women. This must not, of course, be taken to constitute a claim on behalf of women to the credit for the promotion of the new attitude to the problems of poverty, but it cannot be denied that much of the motive force behind it derived from their energies, and that its practical expression was largely determined by them. Certainly the coincidence between what women required of their charitable work and what the new charity required of women was remarkable. Thus the application of scientific method to the solution of social problems fitted admirably with the high regard of women for education, whilst the necessity for professional standards in social work dovetailed with their own sense of inadequacy and their desire for training. The hunger of women to belong to some group larger than the family circle made them instinctive supporters of the enthusiasm for work in groups. Their awareness of the frustrations of their own lives made them so keenly sensitive to those of others that they were quick to accept the new respect for the poor as individuals, whilst their capacity for introducing an emotional quality into a formal relationship fitted most admirably with a concept of charity which in part at least owed its inspiration to the protest against the de-humanising methods of organised charity. In view of all this, it is not surprising to find that the leadership in the introduction of the new approach to charitable work in Liverpool was taken by women.

The earlier generation of "noble matrons" had to a certain extent yielded place to unmarried women such as Florence Melly and Fanny Calder who, whilst they adopted the habitual modesty of their predecessors,[4] nevertheless belonged to the future rather than the past in that they were conscious of a call to public service because of their sex and not in spite of it.[5] However, even they

[4] Fanny Calder is reputed never to have spoken at a public meeting and seldom at meetings of the Education Committee of which she was a member.

[5] At the Women's Conference in 1891, Louisa Twining concluded her paper on Workhouse Nursing with a demand for the appointment of women inspectors and Guardians to deal with the specifically womanly aspects of workhouse administration. *Liverpool Daily Post*, 13th November, 1891.

found themselves in practice excluded from the main stream of charitable effort. Taking flowers to the sick, reading to the illiterate, and teaching cookery to working-men's wives were the types of activity thought suitable for women, and both accordingly turned to educational work as offering them greater scope. Mrs. Rathbone's gesture of herself organising a school nursing scheme and paying for the necessary nurse stands out as a last reminder of the old order.[6] Miss Clough has described the sense of waiting which dominated women of the middle and upper classes in the 'seventies and 'eighties. Some, she said, found the way to emancipation too hard. "Others, on the contrary who were dissatisfied, made up their minds that complaining was vain and unprofitable; they decided that the better course was to be silent, watchful, and alert. They would find their way, but they would be careful not to hurt the feelings and prejudices of those who were nearest and dearest to them. They would keep their strength for the critical moment, and then make the change they wanted. They were quite aware that they might make mistakes, but they hoped that if they tried to be thoughtful and considerate towards their friends, they would be saved from remorse in the future, and they would not bring discredit in the eyes of the world on their careers and doings."[7]

The 'nineties gave them their opportunity. Out of the desperate need of the poor, and the anxiety of the middle classes to do something about them, developed simultaneously a demand and a scope for the services of women far in excess of anything previously experienced. However much men might dominate the administration of charitable societies, the individual act of charity was still regarded as essentially women's work, and women were therefore able to grasp this opportunity without incurring such opposition as had greeted their endeavours to train as nurses or to secure advanced education. Here was work which women both could do and wanted to do, and in which they had no rivals. Personal service was the one thing at their disposal which was really their own to give. Betterment was work with which they were traditionally associated, and for which they had served a long apprenticeship in Ragged and Sunday schools: their own upbringing had been devoted to the inculcation in themselves of precisely those qualities which were now seen to be lacking in the poor. The voluntary nature of charitable work automatically overcame the opposition of those who disapproved of women earning a living, and eased the guilty conscience of women themselves in regard to their revolt.

To women it was as if a door had opened in what they had supposed to be a blank wall. "Was there ever a time when a woman

6 About 1894: responsibility for the scheme was handed on to the District Nursing Service in 1902, and ultimately to the local education authority.
7 Clough, *op. cit.*, p. 254.

could better live than now? Was there ever a country in which woman's position and opportunities were greater than in our England of to-day?"[8] In rapidly increasing numbers, they entered upon their new occupation of voluntary social work. Indeed, the increase in the number of women in relation to that of men is a most striking feature of the charitable scene at this time. Many were women who had secured for themselves some share of the wider education now available in girls' schools and colleges, but the change in emphasis from money to service as the basic qualification of benevolence also brought into social work many members of the middle classes who had previously experienced neither the opportunity nor the urge to undertake practical philanthropy.

The talents they brought to the service of the poor were as mixed as their motives in bringing them. To many, personal service and opportunity were simply different ways of saying the same thing: the result was an astonishing medley of individual ambition and missionary zeal. Women appeared on committees where they had never sat before; they hired rooms in which to run girls' clubs; they painted flowers on the panels of the cupboards at the Domestic Mission; they spent their allowances on pianos for the poor instead of on repairs to their own boots. A Liverpool Union of Workers among Women and Girls was formed in 1890, one of the first such associations in the country.[9] The object of the Union was to encourage sympathy and co-operation between all women engaged in the work of helping and caring for others, and the enthusiasm which accompanied the first Conference held in Liverpool in 1891 is proof of the rare pleasure it then was for women to meet together for any serious purpose. An attempt was made to include working class women in the Conference by holding a meeting specially for them, but this was apparently admonitory in character.

Their world viewed them with astonishment. The *Liverpool Daily Post* doubted if women possessed the necessary strength of will and purpose to live their own lives independently of the usual surroundings of love and care.[10] *The Legion of Honour* commented coldly on the somewhat silly dislike of restraint now displayed by many of the girls of Our Old Families, though *Porcupine* declared stoutly that there was need for an awakening by all good people to the great man and woman question.[11] Whilst the Rev. John Watson of Sefton Park Presbyterian Church, whose influence in directing his congregation into social work was outstanding, said that: "Men are limited as to their work by conditions of sex, temperament, custom,

[8] Miss Janes, speaking at the Conference of Women Workers. *Liverpool Daily Post*, 14th November, 1891.
[9] *Englishwomen's Year Book* for 1898.
[10] *Liverpool Daily Post*, 17th November, 1892.
[11] *Porcupine*, 5th May, 1894.

and education. We know very well what they can do and what they cannot do. The service of women is a perpetually unfolding revelation, an infant science, an unexplored country ".[12]

The women themselves were equally at variance. Miss Ryle, daughter of the first Bishop of Liverpool, declared, when interviewed by *Woman at Home*: "Perhaps you will think me very old-fashioned, but more and more I am getting to think that women are attempting too much in public life. If every woman would do her own duties at home in the way of training her children wisely, caring for and guiding her servants, and using her influence to impart a high moral tone to the social life around her, there would not be the need for all the public reformatory work to which women are now devoting so much of their time ".[13] The interviewer adds somewhat tartly that Miss Ryle evidently failed to realise that as chatelaine of the episcopal palace and her father's private secretary she enjoyed a scope denied to many women. Others compromised by declaring that certain types of work, notably the care of the sick and of children, were inherently womanly: the work of the Kyrle Society in bringing beauty into the lives of the impoverished was regarded as particularly suitable for ladies, and Mrs. Birt advocated the care of orphans as being essentially work for pious motherly women.[14] Many secured for themselves experience of considerable realism under cover of a suitably feminine object. Others, frustrated in social work by conditions which called for political reform, shifted their support to the suffrage movement, earning for themselves the epithet of " platform women ".

It is difficult to decide what effect this influx of women had on voluntary work at this stage. They themselves were well aware of their deficiencies. Miss Janes, speaking at the Conference of Women Workers, on the Self-Education of the Worker, pointed out that their work was inevitably irregular, owing to the sacredness of home ties; that they lacked a grasp of principles and were accordingly liable to do evil in the hope that good might come; and that being primarily ladies, they were offered no alternative to domesticity, which presented them with the difficult task of combining their duty to their people with that care for others to which they would have devoted their whole lives if free.[15] There was about them, however, a quality of almost passionate responsibility towards others on which Mrs. Fawcett commented approvingly.

[12] Sermon to the Conference of Women Workers, 15th November, 1891.

[13] *Woman at Home*. Sarah A. Tooley on " Ladies of Liverpool " (1895). The old Bishop's Palace in Abercromby Square now houses the Department of Social Science in the University of Liverpool.

[14] Smith, *op. cit.*, p. 162.

[15] *Liverpool Daily Post*, 15th November, 1891.

Loan Receipt
Liverpool John Moores University
Library Services

Borrower Name: Griffiths,Jordan
Borrower ID: **********9114

Charity rediscovered :
31111004888523
Due Date: 05/05/2016 23:59

Total Items: 1
14/04/2016 12:31

Please keep your receipt in case of
dispute.

Many were content with the mere fact of giving service, but the more thoughtful and the better educated, and especially those who had inherited the traditions of responsible philanthropy, required more of their work for the poor than the satisfaction of an instinctive benevolence. One of them has described how as a young girl she sat in her father's garden in the then lovely countryside of Egremont, and heard with a deep sense of oppression and responsibility the hum of humanity from the dock-side slums across the river.[16] When a lively intellectual awareness of contemporary thought on social problems was added to such feelings, it is obvious that much of the charitable work offered to women was bound to dissatisfy them. They rejected slumming as lacking purpose and principle. Organised charity appealed to them in theory as providing the "most successful answer to the frustration suffered by men and women of good-will in urban communities when they attempt to exercise the immemorial heritage of sharing with their less fortunate fellow men and find that it is not practical".[17] Nevertheless, in practice the work of a Friendly Visitor proved emotionally and intellectually unsatisfying. The Central Relief Society displayed little of the new respect for the poor which struck such a chord in the hearts of women not yet accustomed to their own improved status. It greeted with no enthusiasm their lively criticisms[18] and their interest in contemporary ideas on social problems: though it consented to a survey of the nature of poverty in 1896, this was limited to eliciting the opinions of the Friendly Visitors.[19]

Not only were new methods not encouraged, but even the old failed to live up to their reputation. The Friendly Visitors were dismayed to find that the utmost sincerity was no proof against the trickery of the scrounger, and that the reformation of the poor required a great deal more than goodness of heart and firmness of principle. William Rathbone pointed out at the Annual Meeting of the Central Relief Society in 1896, that the depressed note struck in the reports from the District Committees might be put down to the fact that they were now realising more clearly the difficulties of the task they had set themselves, and the absolute necessity of careful

[16] Miss Edith Eskrigge in a personal interview.

[17] Frank J. Bruno. *Trends in Social Work.* (Columbia University Press, 1948.) p. 7.

[18] In 1894, while still at college, Eleanor Rathbone read a paper to a group of friends in which she stated that the C.R.S. had made "no permanent, material visible improvement in Liverpool", giving as her reasons the "extremely peculiar constitution of the Liverpool population", the lack of permanent employment for all, and the fact that the C.R.S. scheme was wholly voluntary. Mary Stocks, *Eleanor Rathbone,* (Gollancz, 1949) p. 45.

[19] Published as *The Poor of Liverpool and What Is Done for Them.* William Grisewood. Reprinted from the *Liverpool Mercury,* 1899.

training for it. " Many . . . have a great deal to learn if they are really to do good and not harm."

Meanwhile the exclusion of women from the main stream of charitable effort which has been already noted, had had unforeseen results in that it forced women to seek other means of serving the poor, and so to become pioneers in betterment. The club movement provides the earliest example. It had long been customary for Sunday Schools to extend their work to week-nights simply to keep young people off the streets, and more recently this embryo club movement had benefited from the nationalising of the day schools and the consequent freeing of the services of women who had previously undertaken some form of voluntary teaching. By 1890, when public attention was just beginning to turn upon the possibilities of working with the poor in groups instead of as individuals, enough clubs existed to justify the decision of the Ladies Association for the Care and Protection of Girls[20] to extend the scope of the embryo Union of Girls' Clubs already formed under their auspices. The object of the Union remained nominally that which its name implied, but its real purpose, as of the clubs constituting it, was the opportunity it provided of education in living together. The Annual Competitions held in St. George's Hall, were events of immense importance, but the presentation of the programmes sometimes involved a bitter experience of the art of co-operation as on the painful occasion when a club was recalled for a final marching test after the departure of their accompanist. The club members had almost everything to learn in this respect, and the leaders were almost equally lacking in experience of the give and take of group life. The fact that the members were in worldly experience much in advance of the girls of their own age who came to befriend them added to the difficulty of the work.[21]

However, club work failed to satisfy those who sought to attack the existence of poverty as well as to assist the poor. Quite a number of young women from Liverpool had found in residence in one of the pioneer women's settlements a substitute for college life, and no doubt from their experience came the conviction that to settle amongst the poor offered a possibility of combining the personal service of individuals with a new attack upon social problems as matters for scientific study. There was in addition, a certain appeal in the endurance of poverty, or at least of its near neighbourhood, as a virtue in itself. Accordingly, in 1898, the Liverpool Union of Women Workers stated that : " two ladies offer themselves as heads of a women's settlement to be started in the North end of Liverpool.

[20] Founded 1884 as a branch of the National Association for the Care of Friendless Girls which had originated in a crusade by Miss Ellice Hopkins about 1877.

[21] *Liverpool Daily Post*, 15th November, 1891.

One of these ladies is Dr. Lilias Hamilton,[22] who received her first training (as a nurse) at our Liverpool Workhouse Infirmary (Brownlow Hill) and knows the poor of this city well. The other is Miss Edith Sing,[23] daughter of an honoured citizen of Liverpool, who has prepared herself for this work in Mayfield House Settlement, in London. Convinced that Liverpool is highly favoured by the generous offer of these ladies to become working heads of a settlement, the Liverpool Union of Women Workers wish to promote the scheme by holding a public meeting."[24]

An explanatory note makes it clear that its founders were vague as to the scope and aims of the settlement.

" The primary idea of a settlement is to plant in a centre of vice, squalor and misery, a little oasis of education, refinement and sympathy, to try (to use a Scriptural phrase) to introduce the little leaven which in time—a very long time, of course—may help to leaven the whole lump."[25]

After some difficulty, accommodation was found overlooking the river in that district once known as the lovely retreat of Everton Brow. Now it comprised acres of jerry-built cottages, so closely packed that there was room among them for neither church nor school. Fever was endemic, religious dissension a literal danger. The best that could be said of it was that " no district could offer greater opportunities for work of all kinds ".[26] The settlers moved into a house so decayed that months passed before it was fit for occupation, trying by begging and borrowing furniture, flowers and pictures to create that aura of culture to whose influence such importance was attached: the myth still lingers that the early residents wore formal dress for dinner. Bedroom accommodation for five was available with good sitting-rooms, while the basement was adapted for classes, and for the dispensary which formed the nucleus of the work. Thus once more charity found itself installed in the vacant place of departed gentility, faced with the long struggle of carrying on one kind of work in premises intended for quite another.

The account of these early days reads conventionally enough now. The residents' chief contribution was to act as informed and influential neighbours to the district. The Dispensary and a girls'

[22] Dr. Hamilton was educated at Cheltenham Ladies' College. She had previously held posts in Calcutta and in the household of the Ameer of Afghanistan. After leaving Liverpool, her experiences were various, including the wardenship of Studley Horticultural College for Women. *Cheltenham Ladies' College Guild Leaflet*, LXXXIV, 1925.

[23] Miss Sing was also educated at the Cheltenham Ladies' College. Her father was Joshua Sing, J.P., leather factor, a supporter of education for girls, and a Governor of the Bluecoat School.

[24] Quoted in 1*st Annual Report*, 1898.

[25] 1*st Annual Report*, 1898.

[26] *Ibid.*

club met in the low, ill-lighted basement: help was given with the
Happy Evenings in Board Schools organised by the Kyrle Society,
and "Miss Young read in one of the Tailor's workshops one after-
noon each week". Pioneer work with crippled children had been
begun by the Invalid Children's Aid Society in 1891 under the
auspices of the Kyrle Society. This, too, moved into the basement.[27]
But the mere fact that it was thought necessary to secure the
approval of seventeen patronesses, headed by Lady Frederick
Cavendish, and supported by Mrs. Booth as President, three Vice-
Presidents, and fourteen committee members representative of the
best local families bears witness to the contemporary attitude to
such a venture, especially when undertaken by women.

Changes in Warden were, however, too frequent during the first
few years, and the work suffered from lack of continuity. The Reports
are silent but presumably the Committee was learning by experience
the difficulties of employing women who, though educated up to a
certain point, had not fully accepted the obligations of a professional
career. A salary of thirty pounds a year, with residence, was offered,
but still the position remained unsatisfactory. However, in 1903 the
Committee secured as Warden, Miss Elizabeth Macadam, who had
had experience in various types of club, had trained in two London
settlements, and had already held a professional post as a club
leader. She thus differed from previous wardens in that she had
definitely entered upon social work as her profession. With her
appointment, the Settlement came into its own. Her first annual
report claimed for the Settlement the double purpose of bringing
the lives of rich and poor into a more natural and friendly relation
with each other, and of furthering "the more thorough and scientific
study and treatment of the problem of poverty",[28] to which was
added two years later that "the object of all charitable work should
be to make itself unnecessary".[29]

As one of the few professional social workers then on Merseyside, Miss Macadam was automatically conspicuous, but her energy
of character would in any case have attracted to the Settlement the
considerable number of progressive young women on Merseyside,
whose time and talent otherwise tended to be dissipated. Pupils
from what is now the Belvedere School, and from Cheltenham
Ladies' College were particularly staunch supporters. Mothers aware
of the social propriety of "slumming" sought the Warden's aid in
initiating their daughters, though such recruits seldom exhibited the
staying power of those who came of their own volition, if not
actually in defiance of their family's approval. The best workers

[27] A scheme which eventually led to the opening by the Education Committee of the first Special School in Shaw Street.

[28] 7th Annual Report, 1905.

[29] 9th Annual Report, 1907.

seem to have come from those families so long responsible for leadership in civic affairs, now a closely integrated group, thanks to much inter-marriage and the breaking down of denominational exclusiveness. The most outstanding of these was Eleanor Rathbone, who took an active part in the work of the Settlement, and thus began that long partnership with Elizabeth Macadam which proved so profitable to both.

Eleanor Rathbone was typical of her time and her town. She was able, and her ability was soon recognised. She possessed a trained and intelligent mind. She was a member of that family whose concern for the well-being of the people of Liverpool was proverbial. And she was undeniably a woman. Of all his children, she was the most obvious inheritor of her father's qualities. That blend of principle with practice, that methodical marshalling of facts and resources, that profound and impartial philanthropy, which had characterised his approach to the problems of poverty in his day now reappeared in hers in relation to the problems of the early twentieth century. Like many other women, Eleanor Rathbone found her zeal for social reform frustrated by her lack of political status, and in so far as her life became absorbed in remedying this on behalf of her sex, it is not of immediate concern. Her particular contribution to charitable effort in Liverpool was to infuse the practice of the " new " with the high principles of integrity and social responsibility which she had inherited from her father. Her single-mindedness could prove infuriating, but it revealed a new conception of standards of social work which was of inestimable value to women in their apprenticeship as social workers.

Miss Rathbone's early experience was typical of that of many others. On returning from Oxford, she had volunteered to serve as a Friendly Visitor, and in 1897 was appointed to the North Toxteth committee, of which Florence Melly was secretary. Her influence is at once apparent in the change of tone in the annual reports of the Committee, the directness of style, the statement of fact and statistic, being in striking contrast to that of the other committees, but it was not until Miss Macadam's arrival that she was able to press for the setting up of a model District Committee to give a practical demonstration of modern methods. The Central Relief Society, recognising no doubt that quality in Miss Rathbone's determination which was eventually to make its mark in wider spheres, accepted the scheme as a means of putting into effect their promise to Professor Gonner and the University to provide practical work for students training in social work. In 1904, the Everton District Committee accordingly started work in a room at the Settlement, the only Committee to possess premises of its own. Here, under the direction of Miss Emily Oliver Jones, the theory and practice of modern case work was painstakingly evolved. Careful records were made of every case, weekly discussions of each were held by the entire committee, and the procedure throughout was most carefully planned and supervised.[30]

Thus the old and the new were for a time united. But the lessons of the new were only nervously accepted by the old. They had never understood the necessity for actually living amongst the poor which inspired the Settlement in the first place; they were satisfied that they knew enough about the causes of poverty without making further enquiry; and they regarded experience, especially as a member of a District Committee, as the only training for a social worker. Whereas the Victoria Settlement, in the person of Miss Macadam, stood for precisely contrary views : the poor were the Settlement's neighbours, not their inferiors; their problems called for scientific enquiry with a view to treatment; and Miss Macadam herself was a trained and professional social worker.

Charles Booth's Survey had inspired local imitations but the Settlement was probably the first local institution specifically designed to combine work for the poor with work about the poor, in order that the hit and miss guesses of charity might be replaced by the principles of a science of society. The hand of Miss Rathbone is evident in the consistent collection of material either by the careful keeping of records concerning day-to-day activities, unhappily all subsequently lost, or by the special inquiries instituted from time to time, such as those into the conditions of labour at the Liverpool Docks, and of home and out-workers in the several needlework trades.

The proposed scheme for a training school for social workers has already been mentioned : it constituted perhaps the most difficult to assimilate of all the new ideas for which the Settlement stood. The demand for training in the 'nineties was partly due to the feelings of inadequacy experienced by newcomers to charitable work, and of women in particular, and partly a sign of the increasing appreciation of the complexities of the task of charity in an industrial society. Opinions were mixed as to whether the effect on the true spirit of philanthropy would prove beneficial or otherwise,[31] yet it became increasingly evident that feelings of benevolence were no longer a sufficient qualification for social work. In 1897, a first conference of Friendly Visitors was held, at which Miss Rathbone,

---

[30] Mss. notes by Miss Emily Jones now in possession of the Department of Social Science, University of Liverpool.

[31] Girls' clubs were known to refuse the services of paid teachers of musical drill because their introduction would be contrary to the " spirit of the club ". The Domestic Mission feared that the introduction of a professional element into charity would arouse in the independent Britisher sectarian suspicions and prejudices, while the League of Welldoers was specifically founded to oppose the spirit of professionalism in social work.

newly graduated from Oxford, read a paper on thrift. Such
conferences became annual events, though no formal training
scheme was thought necessary.[32]

On Miss Macadam's appointment, a modest training scheme was
started at the Settlement on the lines of that at the Southwark
Settlement. This gave Professor Gonner, then Professor of
Economics at the University of Liverpool, the opportunity to bring
forward his scheme for a training school for social workers.
Professor Gonner's Address to the Annual Conference of Friendly
Visitors of the Central Relief Society in 1903 reveals that considerable argument was then centring on the subject of training for
social work, whether in a voluntary or professional capacity. His
plea for training was based on the need for increased skill in social
work, for placing the experience of the past at the disposal of the
present, and for providing opportunities for those who could no
longer afford to pursue a vocation for social work in a voluntary
capacity. This last point was, perhaps, his most telling at a time
when more and more women were seeking paid employment, and
voluntary workers were correspondingly hard to come by. To the
argument that training would kill the spontaneous sympathy essential to charitable work, he replied that from " social enthusiasm,
when improperly directed, a great deal of harm may result. It is
evident on all sides ". The Central Relief Society was sufficiently
convinced to accept students for practical work. The Settlement
Committee, equally dubious lest training should undermine the
sense of vocation, nevertheless allowed themselves to be convinced;
the combination of Miss Macadam and Miss Rathbone alone must
have ensured this result!

Had the battle consisted of a straight fight between those for
and those against professional training for social work, its conclusion might have differed. or at least been delayed. As it was there can
be no doubt that the deciding factor was the urgency of the women's
demand for training which would qualify them for the work they
were eager to do. In November, 1904, the Vice-Chancellor reported
to the University Council: "Another development which the
Faculty regards as of much future importance is the University
School for Training in Social work which has been established with
the object of providing an opportunity of systematic study and
training for those engaged, or anxious to engage, in any of the many
forms of social and philanthropic work." Lectures were given at
the University by Professor Gonner, Professor MacCunn and Mr.
Ramsay Muir, who is said to have remarked unfavourably on the

---

[32] The first women appointed to the sanitary staff of the Corporation were
sent to the Society for training, a move out of which eventually grew the
University School of Hygiene. E. W. Hope, *Health At The Gateway.*
(Cambridge University Press, 1931.) p. 103.

presence at his lectures of ladies in white gloves, with Miss Macadam and Miss Oliver Jones as supervisors of practical work.[33]

As a place of residence, the Settlement never rivalled the Southwark Settlement, simply because the much shorter distances between suburb and slum in Liverpool made it too easy for the workers to return home or to be summoned thence. But as a focus of women's activity, it was of the greatest importance. For these educated women had a valuable contribution to make, if only they could find a way of doing so. They may in many respects be compared to the early Dissenters, for they brought to philanthropy wits sharpened by opposition, convictions tried by oppression, and an enthusiasm as informed as it was determined. As their fathers had been before them, they were remarkable in the degree to which they combined the securing of benefits for others with their efforts on their own behalf. Their particular achievement was to give " to the most obscure social worker a new conception of her own significance. She could if she chose become a dual personality. She might be, as she had been ' from time whereof no memory is ', a reliever of human distress, reflecting within a wide or narrow sphere, according to the effective range of her activities, that most excellent gift of charity. At the same time, she might be a researcher; a filler-up of questionnaires; a collector of information of which the minutest item could go to swell the volume of precise knowledge from which an accurate social or economic generalization was distilled ".[34]

It was this combination of the personal with the impersonal, this infusing of the scientific approach of the "new" with the warmth of individual affection, that was to characterise the contribution of women in the early years of the twentieth century. As the last chapter will show, the significance of this contribution lay in the fact that it marked the birth of the conception of charity as social service, and therefore the end of the epoch in charitable effort which forms the subject of this book.

[33] True to charitable tradition, lectures were given in converted premises, this time not of departed gentry, but of Brownlow Hill Lunatic Asylum.

[34] Stocks, *op. cit.*, p. 60.

CHAPTER X

END AND BEGINNING

THE difference of opinion between the old and the new in charitable effort was now becoming plainly apparent, and it was particularly painful to the Central Relief Society in that it found expression in attempts to reform the methods of organised charity from within the ranks of its own supporters. Miss Rathbone, Miss Macadam and Professor Gonner, for instance, used the District Committee for whose work the Victoria Settlement had assumed responsibility, as a means of demonstrating new ideas on relief work, whilst the Toxteth Committee, of which Miss Florence Melly and Miss Rathbone were members, protested in its report for 1902 that: "The drink question, the labour question, and the housing question seem to stand in the way of all attempts to deal effectively with distress, and as years go on certain members of the Committee feel more and more strongly the inadequacy and superficiality of much of their work of relief. In only a very small number of instances have they been able to carry out the instructions to Friendly Visitors, that when relief is given, it should be in such a form as to help those who receive it 'into a position of self-support'. In many cases the relief given serves only to tide the applicant over some temporary distress, which may, and probably will recur."

In reply, the supporters of organised charity could only deplore the effects of both "slumming" and the "new", which they feared must swamp all that they themselves had fought to maintain. Bishop Chevasse's lament that it was easier to find money for charity than deserving cases on which to spend it, the lack of response by the poor to the campaign for inducing habits of thrift, their preference for starvation in their familiar slum rather than migration under the auspices of the Society, all seemed to them to bear witness to a deterioration in the moral stamina of the poor which could only be attributed to the contradiction of their own practice by those who, however well intentioned, worked on fundamentally different principles. They were further depressed by the baffling disparity between the justification of their principles afforded by long years of experience and the lack of any accompanying signs of progress. Mr. Grisewood himself, looking back on his twenty-five years of work with the Society, and asking whether all their efforts had in fact ameliorated the condition of the poor in Liverpool could only claim that "in individual cases we have abundant evidence we have done so, and undoubtedly in many respects a better state of things exist generally, which the Society may have helped in some degree to bring about, not only by its direct work, but by its influence upon public opinion, yet the problem of removing poverty and suffering remains as great as ever."[1]

The fact was that the responsible patronage of the poor by the rich which had provided the basis for the original conception of organised charity, represented the response of a particular period to a particular set of circumstances. The circumstances having changed, a new relationship with the poor, and a new interpretation of the original principles of organised charity, was required. But the supporters of organised charity found it difficult to accept this. Their leaders were not the men their fathers had been. The old breed of merchant princes was dying out: it was said on the death of Mr. H. A. Bright that he was "one of a very few men who still illustrate the possibility of the old connection between letters and commerce",[2] and that with him and his like went that combination of commercial aptitude and moral responsibility which had characterised the Liverpool Gentleman. The old faith had become a matter of habit rather than conviction,[3] and where the fathers had displayed energy and initiative, the sons were only able to summon up a dogged defensiveness.

"Magnificent work has been done in Liverpool by some of the wealthy Unitarian families, but these families are petering out, and the sons are not worthy of the fathers. . . . The present generation of rich folk want to enjoy themselves, find nothing to resist, no class or creed interest to fight for, so that they have ceased to consider anything but their pleasures."[4]

Loyal to the traditions of their founders, the Central Relief Society struggled to apply to the contemporary situation the principle that charity should properly be directed to the relief of the deserving, which in practice excluded from their ministrations all but the helpable. Thus at a time when intemperance was felt to be perhaps the most outstanding social problem, an appeal for Friendly Visitors could be couched in terms which assured them of meeting with no unpleasantness of this nature: "among these people you will find some that are really charming people. . . . We do occasionally find bad and drunken cases; but I would assure those who would like to take up this work, that this Society does not take up drunken cases. I can safely say that in time you get to become really attached to the work which is really delightful work".[5]

---

[1] C.R.S. Annual Report, 1896.

[2] *Liverpool Courier*, 17th May, 1884.

[3] Memorial Service to J. H. Thom. *Liverpool Mercury*, 10th September, 1884.

[4] Beatrice Webb. *Our Partnership*. (Longmans Green & Co., 1948.) p. 162. Written of a visit to her sister, Mrs. Robert Holt, in 1892.

[5] C.R.S. Report, 1906.

This policy reduced the numbers of applicants to manageable proportions, but left unaccounted for a medley of wretched persons whose affairs were the concern of neither the Poor Law nor organised charity.[6] To the Society, the remedy lay in a sharper division of territory between the charitable and the Poor Law. So far as charity was concerned, they reiterated without modification the objects laid down for the Society half a century ago. "The primary object of the Central Relief Society", declared the Manual of Instruction issued to the Friendly Visitors, "is to improve the condition of the poor by raising funds and dispensing relief, by securing due investigation and fitting action, and by repressing mendicity". They felt that their efforts to achieve this were hampered by the increasing and demoralising sympathy of public opinion; a local paper accused them of believing "that the only hope for the poor is the construction of a ring-fence round them to shield them from the careless kindness of the rich".[7] But they also realised that reiteration of the principles of organised charity must be accompanied by a return to the deterrent principles of the Poor Law of 1834 which their own work had originally been designed to complement. It was, in fact, with the secret intention that it should restate these principles that the Royal Commission on the Poor Laws was set up in 1905.[8]

The public being unaware of these cross currents in philanthropic opinion, the announcement of the setting up of the Commission roused no more than a passing interest in the slums. Nor did the publication of its Report attract particular attention when it appeared early in 1909. There was some comment in the local press, but it quickly becomes apparent that the slender public interest in the subject had been extinguished by the sheer bulk of the Report. Even those actively interested in charitable work paid little attention to the fact that its third paragraph specifically stated that this was the first time a Royal Commission had submitted recommendations which proposed not only important modifications of the Poor

---

[6] It is striking to note how often in times of distress the District Committees were able to record that they had been able to deal with all the suitable cases brought to their attention. The number of cases assisted by the District Committees normally only exceeded the number refused by a short head. In 1905-6 the ratio was actually reversed, 920 cases being assisted and 1,084 refused.

[7] Quoted in the Annual Report of the Domestic Mission, 1903.

[8] Webb, *op. cit.*, Chapter 7, p. 322. Beatrice Webb wrote in her diary in December, 1905, of an interview with the assistant secretary of the Local Government Board that besides certain "radical reforms of structure", the Royal Commission was expected "to recommend reversion to the principles of 1834 as regards policy; to stem the tide of philanthropic impulse that was sweeping away the old embankment of deterrent tests to the receipt of relief".

K

Law and its administration, but a revision of the methods of voluntary assistance.

The picture of Liverpool's provision for her poor which emerges from the Report is not a happy one, and it is difficult to believe in face of the silence of the press that many people troubled to read it. What the Minority Report said of the nation as a whole applied with particular aptness to Liverpool: " The nation is confronted . . . as it was in 1834 [with] an ever-growing expenditure from public and private funds, which results, on the one hand, in a minimum of prevention and cure, and on the other in far-reaching demoralisation of character and the continuance of no small amount of unrelieved destitution."[9] The suspicion that the Poor Law and charity, for all their expenditure[10] failed to relieve a considerable amount of distress was confirmed by the answers of the Liverpool Distress Committee[11] to a questionnaire from the Royal Commission, which stated that the majority of the cases dealt with by the Committee were unknown to the Poor Law guardians or the Charity Organisation Society, who were approached in every case before relief was afforded to unemployed families.[12] The only effective co-operation between agencies giving relief to the Liverpool poor was that between the Central Relief Society and the Poor Law, but this concerned a comparatively small number.[13]   On the other hand it emerged that the exceptionally low rate of relief given by the Liverpool guardians was based on the uninformed supposition that the churches and charities would supplement it with relief in money or kind; thus, as the Majority Report put it, balancing inadequate knowledge by inadequacy of relief.

The Commission were unanimous that indiscriminate relief giving by either the Guardians or the charitable public must be stopped, the Minority being particularly outspoken in its condemnation of the " disastrous " effect of the alms-giving of well-meaning persons on the character of the poor and the efficiency of public assistance services. The Majority Report diluted the implied criticism by recommending that recognised charitable agencies should be grouped into local Councils of Voluntary Aid, which

---

[9] *Minority Report,* p. 999.

[10] Which in the case of charity in Liverpool Mr. Grisewood estimated at nearly a quarter of a million pounds annually, exclusive of the considerable poor funds attached to places of religion. Appendix, Vol. IV, p. 64.

[11] Set up under the Unemployment Act, 1905.

[12] Royal Commission on the Poor Laws. Appendix, Vol. xxvii, Cd. 4944. p. 29.

[13] *e.g.* In 1910, a mere 76 cases, involving an expenditure of £174. 18s. 5d. Mr. Grisewood claimed that the investigations of the Society's Officers and helpers were more thorough than those of the Poor Law Officers, and that this justified a system of relief based on voluntary rather than State administration.

would sift all applications for assistance and allow only certain types
to pass on to the Poor Law. The Minority had more positive ideas
on the part to be played by voluntary charity of which more will be
said later.

For a few months after, specialist gatherings such as the
Annual Conference of Friendly Visitors of the Central Relief Society
discussed the findings of the Commission, but the charitable world
as a whole had little conception of the importance, or even of the
relevance to its own affairs, of the downright condemnation of the
old Poor Law principle by the Commission. Indeed, to the Central
Relief Society the findings of the Royal Commission stood for the
vindication of the principles for which they had themselves worked
for so long. Their Chairman claimed at the Annual Meeting that
year that "it was a matter for congratulation that the findings
embodied in the Majority Report were so largely in harmony with
the policy which the Central Relief Society had pursued".
The poor were still to them a permanent feature of society
whose relief was a moral obligation, and willingness to co-operate
with state departments was not allowed to obscure the relationship between rich and poor which this implied. The only
tangible result of the Report was that the Lord Mayor, acting on
the recommendations of the Majority Report, took steps to set up
a Council of Voluntary Aid in 1909 for which the Central Relief
Society supplied the administrative staff, and which was believed
to be the only one of its kind.[14]

Yet though its immediate results might be negligible, the publication of the Report undoubtedly marks a turning point in the
history of charitable effort. From now on, the state was to take over
in a series of legislative acts, the responsibility for class after class
of people whose welfare had till then depended largely on the charity
of their fellow men. Children, the sick, the aged, the unemployed,
were each in turn ensured as of right the help which they had previously enjoyed only according to the dictate and resource of private
philanthropy. Never before had charity faced such a large-scale
transference of territory from the sphere of individual obligation to
that of the community at large: to those whose benevolence ran in
the deep rut of alms-giving, there must have seemed little further
need for their services. At the same time, the improvement in
employment generally, and the better organisation of dock labour
in particular, reduced the amount of material distress, whilst intemperance, long regarded as one of the chief contributory causes of

---

[14] The Council was hampered by the lack of status which either legislation
or the concerted support of charitable agencies in general would have
ensured. Eventually, having taken over from the C.R.S. such functions
as the joint collection of subscriptions, it became the Council of Social
Service in 1935.

poverty, at last showed signs of abating. Poverty was to this extent checked, and the demand for the material help which "charity" could give was correspondingly reduced.

Some societies found it impossible to adapt their work or their workers to the situation, and quietly lapsed, amongst them the District Provident Society within a few years of its centenary.[15] Others came to what terms they could with the intruding state services. The attention of all turned increasingly on the difficulties of finance, although the Royal Commission had been assured that lack of co-operation rather than lack of money hampered the work of charity. This opinion was supported by a survey of voluntary work undertaken by F. G. D'Aeth, Tutor at the School of Social Science, which reported that: "The history of charitable effort in Liverpool reveals the recognition of a number of needs and the establishment of a number of agencies to deal with these needs. The agencies are often started independently and at times differ in their methods of action. This process . . . continued for many years, and in a town notably fertile in its benevolence, has resulted in the production of such a number of independent institutions, and such variation in the methods employed, that some general correlation is much needed ".[16]

This put the case with restraint. In fact, the need of the whole community for learning, or re-learning, the art of living together was nowhere more apparent than in its charitable effort. Objects, methods, principles, were as various and as contradictory as they had ever been. No clear distinction existed between right and wrong in charitable work so that what one society withheld in the interests of the poor man, another gave for that very reason. The high hopes regarding the efficacy of personal service had withered, and it was said that the only appetite roused in the poor by contact with their social superiors was a demand for more, not better things.

Voluntary workers, deeply conscious of inadequacy, were driven to redouble their efforts in a passion of self-sacrifice which all too often became a vested interest. This was particularly true of women, who though they had much to give, expected much in return. "There is no doubt that single-minded interest was the response of a great many people, particularly women, who took up social work in the days before the [1914] war. The work with its vast needs was a greedy absorber of time and interest; in addition it was fascinating and provided a full outlet for personality, sympathy, and organising ability. The opportunities for women to make use of their wider powers were much fewer at this time and social work offered a satisfying means of self-expression, rewarding them also with valuable experience and with human contacts of a very

[15] See p. 30.
[16] F. G. D'Aeth. *Report to the Chairman of the Liverpool Council of Voluntary Aid on the Charitable Effort of Liverpool,* 1910.

real kind: in short, the community needed them and they felt that they could not do enough to respond to this need ".[17]

To analyse the nature of the contribution of such women is not to belittle what has rightly been eulogised in a thousand obituary notices. Women can indeed claim to have kept alive the social conscience at a time when charity had been debased by its confusion with material relief. Nevertheless, they did so at the cost of making social work a feminine prerogative, a process not without penalties.

The truth was that the charitable had for so long been accustomed to bending every energy to the task of succouring those upon whom the Industrial Revolution pressed most hardly, that, inevitably, they were at a loss when that pressure was relieved, even though it was largely by their own efforts that this should have come about. No one seemed to know what charity stood for in the contemporary world. The complexity of social problems seemed to put them beyond the capacity of the amateur, and many baffled people saw no alternative to handing over to the professional worker, and to the state, many of the charitable duties which they as private individuals could no longer hope to fulfil. Perhaps most important of all, there seemed no room in a human relationship based on social justice for the lovely quality of charity whose continued existence the philanthropic had struggled to ensure. Canon Masterman summed up the general feeling when he said bluntly that: "If the existing social order is to be preserved, it must be by clear evidence that the so-called leisured classes are really making a contribution of vital value to the well-being of the community. I believe the principle of voluntary social service is face to face with its last opportunity."[18]

It would be depressing to end on this note, and, more serious, it would be misleading in the extreme. For though "charity" was dead, or dying, that practical expression of man's love of his fellow men which constitutes true charity was already, like a well-pruned shrub, showing promise of new growth at the roots. Voluntary relief giving stood condemned, but both Majority and Minority of the Royal Commission took it for granted that personal service would continue as a permanent feature of social life. They never questioned its desirability and the possibility that it might diminish as a result of the reform of the Poor Law was never even considered. It was in this distinction between material charity and personal service that hope for the future lay.

For though "charity" had had its wings drastically clipped, the need for personal service was never greater. The benefits of mem-

[17] Ireland, *op. cit.*, p. 114.

[18] Address at the Inaugural Meeting of the School of Social Science and of Training for Social Work, 1912.

bership of the new society brought with them obligations which the poor were ill-equipped to meet: their need for education in social living could only be remedied by contact with those of richer experience, and by the organisation of facilities such as clubs and community centres where social skills might be practised. Moreover, the intricacies of the process of securing state aid were often such that the ignorant and illiterate constantly needed advice from those from whom they had previously sought money; indeed, their need for sympathy was quite untouched by the lightening of their anxieties concerning the necessities of life.

The gloom with which the voluntary societies had eyed the future began to lift. They were charmed to find that the extension of state action actually enlarged the scope for individual effort, and the Central Relief Society, for instance, took up advisory work in connection with the payment of insurance money, and of allowances to the dependants of men in the services which ultimately led to the formation of the Personal Service Society in 1918.

The Minority of the Royal Commission on the Poor Laws, convinced that a policy of mere deterrence would prevent neither pauperism nor the warm-hearted generosity of those who hastened to its relief, had proposed that the abolition of the old Poor Law should be accompanied by a deliberate attempt to harness voluntary effort to state services which would nevertheless leave untouched the privilege of the philanthropic to demonstrate the existence of a wrong and the means of remedying it. These proved to be in fact the lines along which charitable effort now proceeded to develop. The theory that one of the main functions of the voluntary agency is to explore and experiment quickly gained general acceptance, but the pattern which the Webbs visualised[19] of voluntary workers within the framework of a state service has only materialised with recent years, the charitable agencies as a rule preferring to receive official grants in aid of their work which leave their previous autonomy untouched.

These were promising lines of development, but perhaps the most significant result of the separation of alms-giving from service in charitable effort was that it made practically possible the precept that charity was not something done by the rich to the poor, but the obligation of every member of the community. This marked a big change. Throughout the nineteenth century, the poor had been exhorted to help themselves, but they had seldom been asked to help others except by such rare people as General Booth. Now, however, the Victoria Settlement reported that " we are glad for the first time to welcome among our helpers some of our working-class neighbours. . . . This is as it ought to be, and we hope more and

[19] Webb. *The Break-up of the Poor Law*. Part 1.. (Longmans, Green & Co., 1909) p. 547.

more that our relation with our neighbours will become that of fellow-workers and friends rather than the old-fashioned one of helpers and helped ".[20] Herbert Rathbone suggested that District Nurses should secure the voluntary assistance of working-class women, to which Miss Eleanor Rathbone added that she did not "think that charitable people in the past have realised sufficiently how eagerly and proudly working women respond to any attempt to organise them as helpers in and not merely the beneficiaries of benevolent undertakings ".[21] The Central Relief Society, although it never so far as is known, appointed any member of the working classes to its District Committees, agreed that the desire to alleviate suffering and to help the unfortunate was undoubtedly universal, equally so with the poor as well as the rich.[22]

There thus began to emerge the new concept of charity which marks the end of the epoch in charitable history with which this book has been concerned. The work of the nineteenth century was done. The past hundred years had seen the disintegration of the system of rights and duties upon which social life had previously been based, and the gradual construction of foundations upon which industrial civilisation might be built. The redefinition of the common basic rights of the individual which this involved, and their interpretation in terms of food, clothing, and shelter, had absorbed the energies of philanthropic men and women throughout this time. Their endeavours had provided a material basis for urban civilisation and the machinery for its administration. The measure of their success was the spate of social legislation which heralded the twentieth century.

The transition from old to new had been long and painful. Men had had to suffer, and learn by their suffering. But how much longer the process might have lasted, how much more profound the suffering involved, not least, how dubious the outcome, had it not been for the saving grace of Victorian philanthropy! "It is easy to criticise this [philanthropic] movement for its incompleteness and its inconsistencies; but if we look back to the England of 1837 with its uncontrolled exploitation of labour, its cities without schools or drains or police, its cholera and its typhus, we shall be astonished not at what was left undone, but by what was achieved by the energy and enthusiasm of the relatively small minority working against the interest and prejudices of an intensely individualistic society."[23]

[20] Annual Report, 1908. The Club Members' Council of 1908 became a self-governing Members' Council in 1947.
[21] *Proceedings* of the Jubilee Congress of District Nursing. Liverpool, 1909.
[22] Alex Mercer. *Charity and Family Responsibility*. Annual Conference of Friendly Visitors, 1904.
[23] *Ideas and Beliefs of the Victorians. The Humanitarians.* Christopher Dawson. (Sylvan Press, 1949.) p. 252.

Yet this was not all, for it was as much the imperishable sense of social obligation as the convinced humanitarianism of that minority of men and women which inspired them to oppose so persistently the individualism and materialism of their times. Through all that long century dedicated to the freedom and the glory of the individual, the charitable stood for a perpetual reminder of man's need to give as well as to receive, to belong to others as well as to stand alone. For all their necessary pre-occupation with material poverty, they never lost sight of the fact that social justice in itself was not enough. Social justice was to them the means to an end, the securing of man's right to "God's natural provision",[24] so that he might fulfil his natural duty of living his life to the glory of that God. Thus Thom, talking of the efforts to improve the lot of the poor which followed upon the 'forties, declared that: " all of these taken together will fall short of what is needed . . . unless through the individual relationships of life, wherever man meets man, there flows the simple, unaffected feeling of Christian regard, the sweetening influence of mutual respect and interest ".[25] In their zeal for science and reason, and their faith in material progress, the charitable may have erred in putting their belief into practice, so that the duty of the rich deteriorated into the giving of material wealth, and the opportunity of the poor man to express his sense of social obligation degenerated into the opportunity to chop firewood at the labour yard. Nevertheless, underneath there always lay the conviction that the ultimate object was to foster in men's hearts " that charity which regards all men as equal, and as such acknowledges that all should be regarded and treated as brothers ".[26] No error of practice could kill this spirit. Though " charity " became cold and formal, true charity lived on in the warm and human relations which developed between innumerable representatives of the middle classes and the poor whom they sought to comfort and befriend, and in the charity of the poor towards the poor which was the redeeming glory of a century of squalid slum life.

It is in the recognition of human relations as the fundamental stuff of charity that the moral of this book lies. Charity is another name for man's need to love and be loved by his fellow men. It is the emotional necessity of community life, without which the welfare state will never become a living society. The reward of true charity in the nineteenth century was the sense it gave of belonging to the community. Charity in the twentieth century is largely deprived of this happy outcome by the lack of opportunity for the individual to give to the state as well as to receive from it. To remedy this

24 Thom., *op. cit.*, p. 156.
25 Thom., *op. cit.*, p. 196.
26 Clough., *op. cit.*, p. 153.

situation is the task which confronts the charitable in contemporary society.

The problem of unexpressed obligations lies at the root of much present-day discontent. Many are unaware of the nature of their frustration: they only know that the receipt of benefits has not brought them the satisfaction they expected. Unless the benefits of the welfare state are accompanied by an equally enhanced sense of obligation and by the development of opportunities for its expression, the danger of the moral degeneration, this time of the entire community, is as serious under the indiscriminate benefit-giving of the state as ever it was under the indiscriminate relief-giving of the rich to the poor.

Florence Nightingale regarded it as her mission in life "to drag the noble art of nursing out of the sink of relief doles".[27] So now must charity also be lifted out of the sink of relief doles, whatever their contemporary guise, and given its proper place as the quality governing man's relations with his fellow men. This is at once the lesson and the legacy of the nineteenth century. If the lesson is not to be wasted, if the legacy is to be put to good use, the charitable of the twentieth century must seek to interpret afresh, in contemporary terms, that "light in the soul, that purpose in the conscience"[28] by which the men and women with whose work this book is concerned, were inspired to make their revelation of divinity.

[27] William Rathbone, M.P. *The History and Progress of District Nursing.* (Macmillan, 1890).

[28] Thom., *op. cit.,* p. 182.

INDEX